TUESDAY
BLUES- DAY

By
Nina Mittman

Tuesday Blues- Day

Copyright © 2025 by Nina Mittman

ISBN: 978-1-969021-33-6 (ebook)
ISBN: 978-1-969021-31-2 (Paperback)
ISBN: 978-1-969021-32-9 (Hardcover)

Table of Contents

Dedication

I dedicate this book to the 26 children in my Fifth Grade Class in 2001-2002 and to the quiet souls of 9/11/2001. Writing this book has been a journey that spanned 21 years.

Acknowledgement

First, I acknowledge my Fifth Grade Class of 26 wonderful 10- and 11-year-olds who actually gave me this story of peace and love after living through a horrific change in the world. I hope that a few of them will somehow read this book.

I also must mention my husband who always encouraged me to complete the book and praised me as a writer. I can't forget my children and grandchildren who inspired me to write this story, and to base the characters on them and their feelings. Last, but not least, to my dearest friend who pushed me several times a year during the 21-year gap between finishing the book in 2004 and publishing it in 2025.

Thank you, all, I did it!

Chapter 1
The Big Year Begins

————⟨℅⟩————

"Dirty, monkeys, smell, completely, bad, really!!! Divide, multiply, subtract, compare, Bring down, repeat!!!!!!!!

"Over and over and over again. Bring down the zero, carry the one, bring down the two, and carry the seven." Jake heard Mrs. Miller's voice going over the steps for long division.

"Okay- okay- focus- focus, Jake. You've got to focus on the board." Jake kept telling himself. But it was really tough to do this Tuesday morning, the second day of his first full week as a Fifth Grader at Franklin Elementary School.

Jake had waited for six years for this year, the year that would make him and his classmates the oldest in the school.

"Role models," as Mrs. Miller had told the class. This was the year of the picnic, the dance, the trip to Broadway to see a

Broadway show and lots of privileges and good things to come throughout the year.

His older brother, Ben, had really loved his year at Franklin as a Fifth Grader. Jake remembered how Ben had always seemed so cool and special, sort of like he was the King of the Mountain! He remembered how envious he had been of Ben, always talking about the special things he could do because he was a Fifth Grader. Now it was Jake's turn. Ben was a lowly Seventh Grader at Rosewood Middle School, and Jake was up at bat! And now the year had come, Jake was going to be king of the mountain, too!

Jake loved school, he always had. He was one of the lucky ones the kind of student who did his work, had some fun doing it, but never really had to overwork himself to get good grades. He would never think of not doing his homework or a report or a special project for school. As a matter of fact, he liked it! It was all part of Jake's plan for success- his goal! His Mom and Dad were always talking about setting goals, being goal oriented, they called it, striving to reach them- plans for this and plans for that. They were always telling both Jake and Ben about their goals, about the way that their "plan" had worked out, only because they had set goals, studied hard, gone to college, and earned good jobs. Jake really did believe them, he knew that they were right about that and he tried to follow along with their rules.

Last year in Fourth Grade, Miss Ringwood's class, he was the Star Student. Jake liked that about himself, but he also liked the fact that he was a good athlete, and the person in the class to be chosen by the kids and by the teacher to do important stuff. When Kazzim had arrived in his class from Afghanistan, Ms. Ringwood even appointed Jake as his mentor, the person to help him through his day and help him with the

English language when he wasn't in his English as a Second Language class.

But not this Tuesday morning! Jake didn't feel like a star student. This Tuesday morning, Jake could have been Dylan Hodges in his class or, even worse, he could have been Vinny Carroll!! Both Dylan and Vinny were okay- but in the smarts department, something had sort of happened to them. Dylan never did a stitch of homework, and Jake could tell that, for all her patience and effort, Mrs. Miller just didn't care for Dylan. And Dylan disliked Mrs. Miller. Vinny, however, was a different kind of kid. He tried so hard that sometimes you thought his brains were going to pop out of his head. He raised his hand all the time, but no matter what, he always got the wrong answers, and Jake felt sorry for him. Most of the class did! Jake's Mom knew Mrs. Carroll from somewhere, Jake couldn't quite remember, but she had told him that Vinny had a learning disability and to be very patient with him. So, Jake felt sorry for him, always imagining some little guy sitting over Vinny's shoulder holding up a stop sign every time Vinny began to answer a question in class. Sort of like one of those school videos they would always see about the body in Health class. The little guy with the stop sign would hold up the sign, and something would happen to Vinny's brain, and he just couldn't answer the question, although he really knew the answer five seconds ago when Mrs. Miller had asked it.

Mrs. Miller was okay- not the nicest of the teachers that Jake had had in school-but she seemed to be coming around. This morning she had actually smiled at the class when they came through the door of her classroom, Room One. "Maybe the heat has gotten to her," Jake thought as he saw the big smile on Mrs. Miller's face.

When the letter from Franklin Elementary School came in the mail in the last week of August, Jake couldn't wait to have his Mom open it to see who his Fifth Grade teacher would be. The bus, the lunch money and all the other stuff in the letter didn't really matter to him, but the teacher did. Each year as soon as the letter was opened, Jake would call his best friend, Andrew Sunshine, to find out who his teacher was, all the while keeping his fingers crossed. The finger crossing thing had worked for five years now, and Andrew and Jake always wound up in the same class as each other. So when his Mom opened the last of the letters from Franklin Elementary, Jake had crossed his fingers, held his breath, and found out that Mrs. Miller, Room One, was his teacher.

"Go ahead, Jakie, "His mother said, "Go ahead and call Andrew before your fingers get stuck together and your face turns blue from holding your breath."

Magic had worked again!! Finger crossing, holding his breath till Andrew answered the phone and all that! It worked again!!

"Mrs. Miller, room one, you and me, again Jake, buddy." "Can't wait to see you- wanna come shopping with me and my Mom? We're on our way to the mall, Mom says I gotta' get some new clothes for school. I'm gonna' get those new cool sneakers we saw, too. Come with us, Days."

Jake thought for a moment, and then realized that he still had to help his Mom with unpacking his camp trunk and duffle. Jake had been away at sleep-away camp in Connecticut, as he had for the past two years. It was sort of a family tradition, Camp Montauk, in the western part of Connecticut. Strange name for a camp in Connecticut, but back when it was opened in the nineteen fifties it was cool to name camps after Native American Tribes, thus Camp Montauk in Connecticut. Camp was always the greatest, and Jake had always tried to talk Andrew into coming along, but Andrew's family went to Nantucket for part of the summer and camp wasn't part of his plan. They really missed each other over the summer, but sometimes it was more fun to catch up on all the news of each other's adventures at the end of the eight weeks. Camp was great, but unpacking, doing laundry and getting everything put away again was not. His Mom never ceased to be amazed at the socks that came home black, the grass in-between the T-shirts and the collections of comic books and other stuff that Jake insisted on bringing back home. So, Jake knew that "Black Laundry Day," as his Mom called it, had to be attended to today. His Mom was home from work today, and she had warned Jake that this would be the day's schedule. Even though Jake always pretended to hate "Black Laundry Day, " it was kind of fun. It was a day his Mom, Ben and he got to spend together, and nothing else interfered with their day. No one came over, it was too boring for anyone else, but they were together. It always seemed that as they unpacked and stuffed the smelly, gooky laundry that came home from camp into the washing machine, each piece led to a story or a memory of what had happened at camp. Pockets were emptied and usually some kind of "treasures" were found along the way, as well. Jake's Grandma and Grandpa lived in California, three thousand miles away from New York, but all summer Grandma sent Ben and Jake letters with dollar bills neatly folded between a tissue, so that they could spend them at the canteen. Sometimes Grandma would send them weird things like bean paste and Tofu cakes, typical California foods, Dad called them, but sometimes she'd break down and mail a package from one of those big discount warehouses with licorice and chocolate and cool stuff. So, when Jake, Ben and their Mom emptied the pockets of their jeans or shorts, they usually found some remnants of Grandma. Thinking about Grandma and Papa Sol always made Jake happy. He was looking forward to their coming to visit soon for Rosh Hashanah, the Jewish New Year. On Black Laundry Day, Jake, his Mom and Ben would have lunch together around the kitchen table or outside on the deck while the washing machine continued to whir and the dryer kept going, all the while Mom complaining "Next year, I'm going to bring it all to a Laundromat and have someone else do this work."

"Can't do the mall with you- sorry, but it's "Black Laundry Day," Jake told Andrew. "Gotta' get all my camp stuff washed and put away today. Mom doesn't have any clients to see today. But come on over here when you get back from the mall, Sunny."

"Yeah, yeah, yeah, Days. Doin' the laundry today. Better you than me. I'll ask my Mom if I can. Call ya' later, Days, gotta' run. Bye"

"Bye," said Jake.

Chapter 2
Best Friends, Sunny Days

So here they were again in room one, Fifth Grade, Mrs. Miller's class, Jake and Andrew, Andrew and Jake, sort of like a team. Best friends, classmates, family friends forever. They both had so much in common with each other that sometimes they thought it was like they were brothers, instead of friends. They were both good students, they both loved to play sports and watch sports. They were Student Council Co-Presidents this year, they each were the youngest in their families and they lived around the block from each other, which was now bike riding distance, since their mothers had started letting them ride their bikes to each other's houses alone, last year. They even had nicknames for each other, which they usually called each other always. Jake was "Days" from his last name Dayman, and Andrew was Sunny from his last name Sunshine.

That's what made them Sunny Days!! Like from "Sesame Street" when they were little. Actually, they didn't mind it, they kind of liked it, "Sunny Days," they were a great team!

Jake looked over at Andrew sitting near the windows and could tell that he was perfectly absorbed in the math review lesson. Jake knew that Andrew was able to divide perfectly, but somehow he had the power of concentration to keep focusing on Mrs. Miller's lesson. Mrs. Miller seemed to be really enjoying herself, too, she was still smiling. Jake remembered hearing his Mom's friend, who was a teacher, say that she never smiled before Thanksgiving. She said that was the way she showed her class how strict she was, and they never took advantage of her. Guess Mrs. Miller didn't learn that in her twenty-nine years of teaching-or she had forgotten it by now, Jake thought.

Mrs. Miller had told the class all about herself on the first day of school, last Thursday, when they had done class introductions. Each kid in the class had to pair up with someone else and interview them. Then, that person had to introduce the class to his interviewee and tell the class all about him or herself. "Sunny Days" didn't pick each other, because they knew it would make them laugh, so Jake had been paired with Mrs. Miller, because the class had twenty-seven kids in it and Jake didn't mind being the odd man out and being interviewed by Mrs. Miller, or interviewing her, himself. Of course, Mrs. Miller didn't tell him the real private stuff about herself. She told Jake where she lived, that she was married for a long time, that she had two grown sons, who both lived and worked in the city, just like Jake's dad did. Jake had even asked Mrs. Miller where her sons worked since he kind of knew the city, having been there so many times with his dad and his Mom, too. But neither of her sons worked at Twin Towers like Jake's dad did. He always loved telling people that his dad worked at Twin Towers, The World Trade Center was actually what it was called, but Jake liked the sound of its nickname better. Twin Towers was a strong and proud name, and it always seemed like something that pleased him to say where his dad worked. Mrs. Miller had even told Jake that she had a cousin who worked at the World Trade Center, but she worked at the big fancy restaurant there on top of the North Tower. Jake remembered that his dad had been there on many occasions.

"Dad," Jake thought to himself as the math problem continued. Jake remembered the promise his dad made to him last night when he came home from the train ride. His dad took the train every morning to the city to work and every evening back home to Long Island. He was usually pretty late, and they didn't get to eat dinner together on a lot of nights, so Jake and his dad did most of their talking while he ate his late dinner and Jake polished off some dessert that he waited for until his dad got home. As they sat together, Mrs. Dayman brought the cold salad with chicken on it to the table for Mr. Dayman. Ben never seemed to want to sit with Jake and his Dad anymore for their dessert-dinner. He was either doing homework or busy on the phone with one of his friends. But Jake still looked forward to their evening ritual.

"No clients tonight, sweetie?" Jake's dad asked Mrs. Dayman.

"No, not tonight, but it's the only night of the week that I don't. Two on Tuesday night after a full day, and two on Wednesday, one on Thursday. Pretty busy week." Tonight I'm going to curl up with a book, relax and just veg out."

Sherry Dayman was a physical trainer. Actually, she herself had worked as a corporate trainer, working for big corporations, running their fitness centers and getting their employees into shape, before Ben and Jake were born. But she had worked in the city, too, at the World Trade Center. That's where she and Jake's dad had met each other; he was in one of her classes. Jake and Ben always thought the story of how their parents had met was a kind of lame. "Too much information," was what Ben would always say.

"When he did his first knee-bend, I knew he was mine," was the way Sherry Dayman told the story.

But when Ben was born, Sherry decided not to commute into the city, it was just too hard. So she opened her own business, got her own clients and was pretty successful. Now she just worked at clients' homes during the daytime hours when Ben and Jake were in school or in the evenings. She usually alternated weeks, so this must have been the week that she also worked in the evenings, Jake thought.

"So, Jakie, boy, how's Fifth Grade? What's happening, what did you do in school today? Things should be rolling now, first full week and all," said Mr. Dayman. "Do tell."

"Okay, here it is," thought Jake. The routine, how is school talk. Not that Dad wouldn't ask him every night, but the beginning of the school year was always different. Sort of like getting the lay of the land. Who's in your class, what's the homework policy, what's the teacher like, what do you need for supplies, and on and on. Not that Jake didn't like talking to his dad about school, he hated to admit that he loved it, loved talking to his dad about anything, but really, they had been over all of this last week on Thursday night, after the first day of school.

"Dad, Gym's gonna start tomorrow, on Tuesday, and I really need some new sneakers for Gym. I have new ones for everyday in school, but I saw the coolest pair, which are really better for Gym. Sunny got them, and I really need them, Dad."

"Need, Jakie, or want?" Asked Dad.

"Want, Dad, want them a lot," said Jake.

Dad and Mom had spent lots of time explaining to both Ben and Jake about the difference between needing and wanting, and Jake got the concept. He knew that money was never an issue for his parents. They had all the money they needed for everything. However, they always wanted to ensure Ben and Jake were not spoiled, as they called it. Jake always imagined Ben and himself as two big pieces of meat, lying in the sun, spoiling, when his dad and Mom had "the talk" with them. But he really knew what they meant, and he knew how lucky he was. He had been taught to appreciate what his parents could give him. He really never took the things he had for granted, never bragged or showed off, but most of his friends had the same things he had, anyway. Sherry and Marc Dayman made sure that their children appreciated what they had and thought about others in the world, who were not as privileged as they were. Giving to charity was important to them, and they made sure that Jake and Ben understood that. As a Jewish family, they worked in the soup kitchen that their Temple had on Christmas Eve, every year, to help the needy families in their community.

"Well, Jakie, I can't get them for you for tomorrow, but you can have them for the next day you have Gym. Okay, Jakie, tell you what. Since Mom is working tomorrow night, I'll take you for the sneakers you want then. I'll work it into my schedule, and I'll come home early on Tuesday night. We'll see if Ben wants to come, and the three of us will have dinner on the way to the mall, then we'll go get you those sneakers that you "need." Dad said as he winked at Jake.

That's what made his dad so easy and cool to be with, Jake thought. "Awesome, Dad. Thanks."

"What do you want for dinner, Jake?" Dad asked.

That was never hard for Jake to decide. It was a no-brainer.

"Pizza, pizza, dad."

Pizza was Jake's favorite food, anytime of day, day or night, pizza!! He even ate it cold for breakfast right from the refrigerator, although it didn't make his Mom happy.

"Promise, Dad? Do you promise you'll really come home early on Tuesday night?"

Jake worried that, as so many nights before, his dad would promise to come home early, but even though he meant it with all of his heart and would never really break a promise to Jake or Ben, something at work would come up. Something would go wrong with the "market" as Dad referred to the Stock market, and Mr. Dayman would have to stay at work late. He often explained to Ben and Jake that all the things they had together and all the things they did together came as a result of his hard work, setting goals, and having a very important job in the "market." That his and Mom's hard work paid off and that's what gave Jake the opportunity to be at summer camp, for their family to do all the great things they did on the weekends together and live in such a nice house. But sometimes Jake just didn't care, even though he really understood. Dad would never just not show up, he'd call from the office or his cell phone, but even though he understood, Jake would feel really disappointed anyway.

So that was how the arrangements had been made. Tonight, was the night that Jake would get the coolest sneakers ever put on Earth. No big deal that he wouldn't have them for Gym today, he'd have them on Thursday, but he couldn't stop thinking about getting them at the mall tonight.

Chapter 3
The Sneakers and the Promise

This morning when he came downstairs for breakfast, he reminded his Mom of the "promise" that Dad had made to him the night before.

"Mom, did Dad remember coming home from work early tonight, did he say anything to you about it?"

"Yes, he sure did, Sweetie. He said he'd be on the Four-thirty- four train. You know he never forgets about promises he makes to you or to Ben. He'll be here and you'll get those sneakers. Stop worrying, Jake, come have breakfast before it's too late. Your cereal is on the table. It's such a beautiful day. Feels like it's still summer, doesn't it? Here we are, September eleventh, and it's seventy-three degrees out already, and the sky is a perfect robin's egg blue. What a great day. Don't you just love days like this, Jake?" His Mom smiled at him as she poured herself a cup of coffee in her favorite Buckeye mug.

Ben wasn't paying much attention to either of them as he continued to eat his bagel, kissed Mom goodbye, and ran out of the door, kind of late to catch the bus to Middle School.

"Yeah, it looks pretty nice out, Mom. Are you sure Dad will be home early enough to take me?" asked Jake.

"Jake, he will. He will. Now go, or you'll be late. I have to get out of here, too."

So here he was, Tuesday morning, in school, unable to focus, unable to concentrate, unable to think about anything except the new sneakers he was going to get. One more looks out the window, he thought to himself. Yeah, Mom was right, it was a beautiful day, and that was part of the problem, it just didn't feel like school weather. It felt like summer, and he was going to get his sneakers on this beautiful, absolutely gorgeous sunny Tuesday.

Focus, focus, he thought to himself, Mrs. Miller was surely going to call on him soon. She'd probably call on him when the problem got harder, because she knew that Jake would be able to do it. Teachers always did stuff like that. Sometimes they called on you when they knew you weren't paying attention at all, just to shake you up and get you to concentrate. Jake always felt sorry for the kids who were called on them and couldn't answer, because they really didn't understand. But Jake knew that he could sort of daydream and still know what was going on up on the board. So, he put his eyes back up there, and "checked the division problem out" with Mrs. Miller. It was a good thing that he did because just then she said that they were going to have a quiz on ten division problems to see who still needed review from Fourth grade and who could go on without the review. Jake felt sort of happy that the quiz would force him back to the classroom "reality."

Mrs. Miller began to write the problems on the board as the class copied them. Just as she finished writing, the telephone in the classroom rang. Most schools didn't have telephones in their classrooms. Jake had found that out when he and his camp friends always talked about school. Some of his friends had televisions built right into their classrooms, though. He had always thought that would be much cooler than having a telephone. After all, the TV could be used to watch videos without having to wait to sign up for the video monitor like his teachers did. His camp friends had told him that sometimes they even got to watch important things on TV in the classroom, like when the President was inaugurated, or when the votes were being counted and recounted for the 2000 Presidential election, last year in Fourth Grade. But no, his school had telephones in every classroom that could receive in school or out of school calls and make them both also. Sometimes when teachers were really angry or needed to speak to a kid's Mom or dad, they would just call them right from the classroom in front of the class. Jake always thought that this wasn't really right, but some of the teachers did it anyway. It was always hard to listen when the teachers got calls, they spoke on the phone softly, and the class could never really hear them. They would walk with the receiver out into the hall, because all the phones were on the walls near the doorway of the classrooms. The kids could always tell if the call was "personal" or for school, because if it was for school, like the office calling, the teachers would talk in their "teacher" voice on the phone. But if they got a call from "home," they would always lower their voices and walk into the hallway. Most of the teachers had a "phone monitor" as a classroom job. This was a job that everyone always wanted, Jake thought it probably made everyone feel important and besides it usually let you know who was calling, because the teachers, as Mrs. Miller had, always insisted that the phone monitor answer the phone by saying, "Mrs. Miller's classroom, this is Suzy Q speaking, who is calling, please?" Whenever Mrs. Miller had to substitute a real name for a fake name she said "Suzy Q." She must have thought that was really funny, because she seemed to laugh whenever she said it. Mrs. Miller was nice enough, but it seemed like she was close to Jake's Grandma's age and she had the same sense of humor.

So, the phone rang, but Mrs. Miller said, "I'll get it, I'm right here, work on the quiz, children." And she went to answer the phone herself.

Chapter 4
The First Challenge

Jake went to work on the division problems, now that he had finally put Dad and the cool sneakers out of his mind, for a few minutes, at least. He didn't even have to think about "Dirty monkeys smell completely bad, really." (Funny how he could never forget it- the way to remember divide, subtract, multiply, compare, bring down, repeat!) He would just work on the math quiz, ace it and feel proud of himself.

As he worked on the first problem, he was aware that Mrs. Miller was "out in the hallway" with the phone, the way the teachers always did when the calls were "from outside of school." He knew that he wasn't the only one in the class "half listening" to her, but she couldn't really be heard. Mrs. Miller was on the phone for a few minutes when Jake was on the third problem, and she hung up the phone and went immediately over to her desk. The only reason that Jake and some of the other kids were aware of what Mrs. Miller was doing was because she didn't walk around the class and look at all the kids and their work to see what problem they were on and how they were doing. Teachers always did that, and even though they had only been together as Fifth Graders for five days now, Mrs. Miller had done it, too. She was definitely a teacher who was interested in what her students were doing and would always follow her own rules. Jake could tell. But she didn't, and it made Jake think that she was acting strangely. Out of the corner of his eye, he saw Mrs. Miller reach into her big purse and take out her cell phone. It was so quiet in the class that he heard her turn it on, too. Everyone had a cell phone, his Mom, his dad, everyone he knew, even some of the kids had them so their parents could always get in touch with them, but they couldn't use them in school! He had never seen one of the teachers actually use her cell phone in school, so he thought it sort of odd, but he went right back to doing his math problems on the quiz. Maybe Mrs. Miller had something important to do. Jake thought to himself how lucky he really was that he could do his math and look around the room and think about Mrs. Miller, all at the same time. He was always able to do that, concentrate on several things at a time. He looked around the room and saw that Andrew had noticed Mrs. Miller, too. Andrew gave Jake a kind of shrug, meaning, "What's up?', but when Jake shook his head, they both went back to the math work.

"Keep working, boys and girls," said Mrs. Miller as she went back to the front of the room, to the classroom phone and out into the hall with the cord. "I need to make a call, but I'm watching you, do your best." That was all Mrs. Miller said, and then she was on the phone again, facing out into the hall.

"Wow," Jake thought to himself. "Mrs. Miller is as distracted as I am, today. Maybe she's going to get new sneakers tonight and have pizza, too." That thought kind of made him smile to himself as he looked back at the math and then over to the door where Mrs. Miller was standing again. But something seemed weird, strange, and unusual. He could see that his teacher had put her cell phone into the pocket of her skirt, as she came back through the doorway. Now she walked to the back of the classroom, where the outside wall was and took the phone out of her pocket and began punching in numbers! Jake had a great imagination, and when he was bored, he loved to imagine things and make up stories. He'd make up funny situations in his mind. Maybe Mrs. Miller is really an alien sending messages back to her mother ship, he thought and smiled to himself.

"Really strange," thought Jake. And he noticed that he wasn't the only one watching now, either. Some of the kids were looking at her, and Mrs. Miller didn't even seem to care. She had the cell phone up to her ear, but Jake guessed that she couldn't reach the person or alien she was trying to get, because she shook her head and put it back into her skirt pocket.

Mrs. Miller walked back up to the front of the room and right outside into the hall. Now Jake knew that teachers always did that to talk to another teacher or to someone passing by in the hallway, but Mrs. Miller acted like she was on a mission, and her face didn't look too great, either. She looked worried, and not about the division quiz.

Jake kept working on the math quiz, as most of the class did. They were really a good class. That's what Mrs. Miller had kept telling them for the first five days of Fifth Grade. He had wondered if she just did that to make them all feel good about themselves or if they really were just a good combination of kids. They must've been, Jake thought, because even though they were all aware of Mrs. Miller and her phone calls, they all kept working. Not like last year when Miss Ringwood would turn her attention away from the class and someone would burp or talk or make faces. Miss Ringwood didn't know how to handle it, but Jake suspected that they all knew that Mrs. Miller did and would, so they were all good, all of the time, except maybe for Dylan Hodges.

Jake was just checking the last problem by multiplying the quotient times the divisor, as he had been taught back in third grade, when he heard Mrs. Miller in the hallway. She was talking to Mrs. Petrie, one of the other Fifth Grade teachers, but they were sort of whispering. Jake thought that Mrs. Petrie didn't look too good, either. Was she going back with Mrs. Miller on that spaceship?

Now Mrs. Miller came back in, went back to the back of the room and tried her cell phone again. She shook her head again, and went back up to the classroom phone, looking worse than ever. He could hear her this time, though, as if she didn't care, and she left a message for someone on their voicemail to call her. He didn't know who the "someone" was, but she sounded really desperate to talk to him or to her.

"Please call me at school or on my cell phone. Why aren't you answering your cell phone? Bye." Jake was able to hear Mrs. Miller pretty clearly.

Jake looked around the class and, except for Vinny and a few others who were struggling on the quiz, it seemed as if everyone in the class was watching Mrs. Miller now. Mrs. Miller looked like she had seen a ghost!! Not even Jake's mind could come up with a fantasy to explain Mrs. Miller's actions. Jake couldn't possibly think of what could have happened. It seemed as though everyone in the class was watching her now. Just as Jake was looking at Andrew, trying to get his attention, Dr. Snow, the principal, came to the doorway of Room One. Whatever was wrong, Dr. Snow looked like it was wrong for her, too. When she appeared at the doorway to speak to Mrs. Miller she looked like she had been bitten by the same bug as Mrs. Miller and Mrs. Petrie had!!

"Oh, shoot," they're going to whisper again. What are they all whispering about? thought Jake. "What could possibly happen at Franklin Elementary School on Long Island in September?" He remembered his mother talking about a hurricane way before he was born that "hit" Long Island and closed the schools for a whole week!! He heard his Mom say that she was in college then, and hadn't gone back to Ohio yet, and it had really caused a mess. Last year in Science they had done a weather unit and even talked about hurricanes. "Yes!" he thought, "A hurricane in September could be a real possibility. Oh, no, not tonight, not tonight when it was Tuesday, sneakers and pizza!"

Chapter 5
Strange Signs

Jake didn't even really know what it would be like to be in a real hurricane, but he could bet that the Long Island Railroad would be late, something that his family was used to, and that his dad would never make it home in time to get to the mall with him and Ben. "Please, no snowstorms, heat waves or hurricanes." He thought to himself, but he was almost saying it out loud, when Mrs. Miller came back into the classroom.

"Boys and girls," she said. Please stop working on your quizzes and pass them to your table monitors.

"Mrs. Miller, Mrs. Miller, I'm not finished with the quiz, well, not really anyway, I haven't checked it, and…" said Danielle Reese, squirming in her seat. She didn't even stop to take a breath; she was so nervous about not completing her quiz! Jake knew Danielle since Second Grade and she was always in a state of panic. Danielle seemed like she was more serious and intense than any adult that he knew. She also always had an opinion or knew something about something or someone, and she was never afraid to say so.

"Danielle, relax, don't worry. We'll finish it another time if we have to. Just hand in your papers, children, I need to talk to you."

"Oh no, here it comes," thought Jake as he looked around the room. He had finished and checked his quiz, but what was going on? When the Table Monitors had all brought the papers up to Mrs. Miller, she placed them on her desk, never looking at them, which was also very unusual for her, and went to the front of the room.

Mrs. Miller had that serious, but not angry look on her face, like she was going to tell the class that they hadn't been working hard enough, or that school was a very serious business, that it was their job, just like their parents had jobs. That was the kind of speech that teachers always made with that serious look on their faces. But Mrs. Miller looked different. Jake couldn't quite put his finger on it, but she was acting weird! Maybe it was the hurricane, after all.

Mrs. Miller went to the door of the classroom and closed it. She never, ever closed the door. She had told them that on the first day of school last week and also said that closing the door made the classroom even hotter than it was. But not now, she had closed it!

"I guess she wants to keep the hurricane out of the room," Jake imagined.

"Children," said Mrs. Miller. Jake could tell that she still had her cell phone on because she kept feeling for it in her pocket. "Children, I need to speak to you about something. Firstly, Dr. Snow has told us that we are in what is called a "lockdown." What that means is that we are to close the classroom doors, and not leave the room, unless you have an emergency and need to use the bathroom. If you do, as usual you will take the bathroom pass, but you must leave the room only with a partner. You are not to leave the room without my knowing or alone. Now, I know that you don't understand this, and I wouldn't either if I were in your place. So...I'm going to do something that I am not supposed to do at all. Please push in your chairs and come to the front of the room, let's sit on the floor around me in the Literature Corner."

All the children in the class did as Mrs. Miller asked, and they did so quietly, as if they were going to hear some startling news. Jake thought to himself that they would be told that school was closing early or something. He wondered if school would close early for a September hurricane.

"Children," Mrs. Miller said softly. I have been told not to tell you what I'm going to tell you, but I have decided for myself that since you are the oldest students in the building and since I truly believe that you can't understand what's going on, unless I explain it to you, I am going to go against the rules and explain to you what has happened this morning. I promised you on the very first day of school, last week, that I would always treat you fairly, honestly and with respect. Do you remember that?"

Everyone shook their heads to mean yes to Mrs. Miller. Jake did remember that little lecture from her last week and actually had gone home and told his Mom about it because it made him feel sort of grown up and happy that Mrs. Miller was his teacher. Jake had always been treated that way at home and enjoyed the fact that his teachers shared that philosophy.

"And, boys and girls," added Mrs. Miller, "I'm sure that you also remember that I said if you were cooperative and did your best we could all have a very respectful classroom, where we could all feel free to express ourselves and share with each other, while helping each other. Well, that is what I am going to do. But this has to be our little secret for now. When you get home today, you can certainly tell your parents what I told you, but for the rest of the school day, I would prefer that you not tell any other students what I will be telling you. Is that clear?"

"Whew, it can't be a hurricane because everyone would know about that, even the kindergarten children. So, no hurricane, thank goodness, pizza and sneakers are on!" thought Jake.

"Something truly terrible has happened today. I really don't know as much about it as I'd like to, but what I do know right now, without the help of a television or a radio, I will share with you. I know that you are all aware that I have received and made several phones calls this morning." Mrs. Miller paused and looked each and every one of the children square in the eyes.

"The phone calls," Mrs. Miller continued, "were from my family…" Mrs. Miller felt for her cell phone again, and said, "The first call was from my older son, Harrison. He works in the city for a big magazine. He works in midtown Manhattan. Uh, it uh seems that an airplane went into the Twin Towers this morning, just about an hour ago, a little before nine o'clock am."

Pause, pause, pause…." And, um, it seems as if uh, it's pretty serious, but we don't know just how serious it is. Actually, uh, Harrison, my, uh, son, was especially worried because we have a cousin who is his very close friend, who works at the restaurant there at the top of the Twin Towers. His second call was to tell me that my younger son, Adam, was all right, as is Harrison's fiancé, - they all work in the city. Now most important is that I don't want any of you to worry, but I have noticed cars pulling up into the school driveway and some parents are picking up their children and bringing them home. That's one of the reasons that led me to my decision to tell you. I guess they just feel better about doing that. But I want you to know that you are perfectly safe here in school, and that we are in no danger. It's just that Dr. Snow doesn't want us wandering around the building, you know like in a fire drill or something like that. So, relax, take it easy and I promise you that as soon as I know something more, I'll let you know."

What in the world was Mrs. Miller talking about, thought Jake to himself. A plane into the World Trade Center? Was it just hanging there, sticking out of the building like some weird video game on his computer? How could an airplane not see the Twin Towers? Which one, which tower was Mrs. Miller talking about? Jake wondered if his dad could see the plane from the window of his office. Maybe the news was going to be there. Oh no, Jake thought again to himself, I bet this will put Dad on a later train. Any time something happens, the trains are late coming into Long Island.

Mrs. Miller continued to look at the class as if she was waiting for them to do something, but no one really knew what to do. Jake had made a mental picture of what he thought had happened at the Twin Towers, just as Danielle Reese raised her hand again.

"Mrs. Miller," Danielle said in her most serious and panicked tone. "I don't really understand exactly what it is you are saying to us. After all, my uncle is an air traffic controller here in New York and he once told me about the computers and all the technology they use, actually it was when my family was going to Disney, and uh, I was rather nervous because it was my first time flying, and uh, my uncle told me how very safe it is. So, I don't know what you mean, you mean a really little plane went into the Twin Towers?

Which one, Mrs. Miller, and how? How would that happen? It doesn't make sense to me at all."

Andrew raised his hand now. "Yes, Andrew, you have a question?" answered Mrs. Miller.

"I keep looking out the window, Mrs. Miller, and I keep seeing more and more people's parents coming to school and picking them up, and Sarah, Glenn and David were already picked up from our class...so where are they all going and why are they going and also my dad works near the Twin Towers, do you think he could've seen it? "

All of a sudden hands went up all around the group on the floor. Everyone seemed to have something they needed or wanted to say. It was like everyone in the class had the same thought and needed to ask questions all at once.

"Andrew, those are very good questions. I'm not sure that I am able to answer any of them for you. Remember, I am here in this classroom, just as you are. I don't really have any other outside information. I suppose that some parents are feeling uncomfortable for their own reasons and just thought it best to come to school, but as I previously told you you are safe here at school.

Safe? safe? Why does Mrs. Miller keep talking about being safe, Jake thought? Why wouldn't we be safe, why would an airplane going into the Twin Towers miles away have anything to do with our not being safe, and why did Mrs. Miller seem so upset all morning? Did her son always call her to let her know what was going on in the world outside of school? Maybe that was an arrangement they had with each other. Maybe Harrison was Mrs. Miller's on the spot newscaster. No, thought Jake, no, I don't like the sound of this. But if something were really wrong, Mom would leave her clients and come to school for him. Jake felt secure in that thought as Mrs. Miller continued to answer Andrew's question.

"Andrew, dear, I wouldn't know if your father would have seen the plane. Maybe when you go home, you'll have your answers. We all will. Now let's try to refocus ourselves on our class work. I'd like you all to go back to your seats and take out your independent writing and write for a while. While you are doing that, I will go over to the computers and go online and see what I can find out. Please relax, children."

Chapter 6
Whispers and Worry

——————⟨⟩——————

With that the class went back to their seats and it was really strange, but everyone got right back to work. All of a sudden Mrs. Miller's class had turned into a group of little authors, all writing away as if they couldn't wait to get their thoughts down on their papers. All except, Dylan Hodges that is, who shouted out.

"Hey, dudes, here comes a plane right at school, I think it's heading for our classroom!" he laughed out a huge, heh, heh.

"Just kiddin', folks, just kiddin'!"

"Dylan, I don't think that was an appropriate joke," scoffed Mrs. Miller, "and I would appreciate it if you would also get to your writing. We all need to cooperate with each other, Dylan, dear. Let's try to do that."

Dear? Dear? Mrs. Miller usually called the children in the class, "dear," it was a sort of sweet and corny, but Jake didn't mind it, but she never called Dylan dear, there was nothing dear about Dylan, not to Jake or to Mrs. Miller. Why was she calling him dear now of all times when he was calling out and being a jerk?

Mrs. Miller went back to the computers at the back of the room. Every morning when the class came in, the "Computer Monitor 'booted up the computers and left them on to be used throughout the day. Jake hadn't noticed if anyone had used them this morning, but he didn't think so. Mrs. Miller kept going from one computer to another, and she didn't seem to be too successful.

"That's strange, Mrs. Miller said almost to herself, but loud enough for everyone to hear her. "I can't seem to get online. I guess the School District network is out, it just keeps saying, this page cannot be displayed. Well, so much for getting any news. "Then Mrs. Miller said, "It's time for Gym, please straighten up your desks, and line up quietly for Gym, boys and Girls, and remember, no discussion of our little "talk "outside of this classroom." Jake thought Mrs. Miller sounded as if she had shared some very privileged information with them.

Some of the girls, Danielle, Cassidy and Crystal all shook their heads and looked at Mrs. Miller. "We remember, Mrs. Miller," said Cassidy. "Don't you worry."

Yuck, thought Jake. Why are they always like that? Kissing up to the teacher. That's what girls were always like in school. Even the best boys, including Jake and Andrew, and Sean, would never think of acting that way. Oh well, he thought, who cares. Jake loved Gym and kept thinking about getting those cool new sneakers tonight and spending some time with his Dad. He did hope that the pilot in his little plane was okay, though.

Chapter 7
Lockdown and Confusion

Gym was okay and they were really just doing beginning stuff, going over rules of the gymnasium, line- up and all that other stuff that they began with every year. As a Fifth Grader Jake and the rest of the class knew all the rules, but they had to hear them again, anyway.

The whole school seemed strange though. Jake couldn't really put his finger on it, but he felt like something was different and odd and more than Mrs Miller had said to the class. Phys Ed class was always with another class, sometimes two depending on the schedules. This year they had gym with Miss Sullivan's class. They were Fifth Graders, also, and Jake and Andrew's friend Paul was in Miss Sullivan's class. As soon as they were standing near each other in the Gym, Paul began whispering to Jake.

"Jake, did ya' hear? About the attack on the Twin Towers?" Paul looked like he was about to tell Jake that his favorite team had just won the Super Bowl.

Thinking about what Mrs. Miller had told them made Jake queasy inside. And yet he wasn't supposed to talk about it to anyone other than his classmates in Room One. Jake looked at Paul, shook his head, and replied.

"No. No, I haven't. But don't even think that, Paul, let alone say that! That's an awful thing to go around saying! Shhh. Mr. Simon is looking over here at us. The last thing we need is to be on his bad side. Shhh!"

Mr. Simon continued on with the rules of the Gym, the class and what the Fifth Graders were going to be doing this year. But Jake just couldn't concentrate on what he was saying. And Jake thought to himself, that Mr. Simon was actually acting pretty weird today, too. He knew that he had seen Paul talking to Jake, but he didn't even say anything or give them "the look." "The look" was what teachers did when they wanted to give you a warning, or if they were really strict teachers, they could give you "the look" and it was really worse than saying anything to you, at all. Mr. Simon ran a really "tight ship," as he called it in the Gym, but he was acting weird today, like everyone else. Jake began to think that Mrs. Miller really wasn't telling them everything that there was to know. He decided that when they got back to class and had their five-minute snack time, he would ask Andrew what he thought and then they would decide what to do.

When they got back to the classroom, while having snack, he asked Andrew what he thought.

"Sunny, I'm nervous. You know what Danielle said. And didn't you see what was going on in the lobby? So many Moms and dads are here. Even Mr. Simon was acting weird during Gym, and the teachers are all talking in little groups and I don't know. Do you think Mrs. Miller told us the truth? Do you think she knows something else? Paul said that there was an "attack" on the Twin Towers! I'm getting really nervous. I know this sounds really lame, but I wish my Mom would come for me so I could go home and watch TV and see what's going on. I feel spooked!"

Andrew replied, "Days, what's there to worry about? Relax. You heard Mrs. Miller. If something was wrong your Mom and my Mom would've been here to pick us up. It's mostly the little kids that went home; their Moms get worried about them."

"Sunny, let's ask Mrs. Miller. She said she'd be honest with us; I'm going to ask her." With that they heard Mrs. Miller tell them to return to their seats. Jake looked around the classroom at his friends and classmates and he realized that some others had left during Gym class. He felt nervous and he sensed that some of the others in the classroom felt the same way. He looked over at the computers in the classroom and saw that they weren't even on! Mrs. Miller had told them that she would "get the news" online! The computers were still all dark. That was really odd!

Chapter 8
The Missing Link

When Mrs. Miller appeared in the front of the class again, she looked even worse than she did before. Today was such a beautiful day, Jake thought. The sky had been clear blue all day, and it felt like a perfect summer day, even though it was September 11th. But September 11th was turning out to be a strange day, Jake thought, and he didn't like what he was thinking. Just as Jake had put his hand up to ask Mrs. Miller his question, Mrs. Miller began.

"Boys and girls. I am not able to access any information for you on the Internet. It seems that everything is out. The internet is not working, nor are the cell phones. Actually, the lines here at school are working, but the secretaries in the office told me that so many people are calling, that all the phone lines are busy and no one can get out or in on them. So, I really don't have too much information for you, except that there are some rumors going around. It does, however, seem that the damage to the Twin Towers is serious. Now that doesn't mean that it is an attack, or that we are in danger."

Mrs. Miller took a deep breath as if she were going into a yoga position like his Mom did and smiled gently at the class again. Jake thought that she looked like they had all failed the biggest test of their lives, and she felt sorry for them that they might all be doomed to stay in Fifth Grade forever.

"I can tell you that many years ago before you were all born, if you can believe it, when I was a little girl, a plane also went into the Empire

State Building. If I remember correctly, the pilot misjudged and went into the top of the building, on a foggy morning, of course, back then, it was the tallest building in the world. Everything was all right, and the Empire State Building still stands gracefully against the New York City skyline. I think what we should do is try to take our minds off this. I'll give you a choice; you can work on any piece of work that you want. You can work on reading and answering your comprehension questions, you can take your math back or you can work on your Document Based Questions for Social Studies. You can even work in your Cooperative groups. How's that?"

"Oh, Jake, I'm sorry. I forgot that you had your hand up. What is it dear?"

"Mrs. Miller," Jake began, "I don't want to seem rude, or anything, but I've noticed some strange things going on in school. So many kids are getting picked up early, and so many teachers are talking quietly to each other, and someone even told me that there was an attack or something. I don't get it, but I'd really like to know. My dad works at the World Trade Center, in the Twin Towers. Uh, he was coming home early tonight, and I'd like to know what's happening. Isn't there some way we can find out, Mrs. Miller, please." Jake had held his breath through his long question, and now it was all out. He put his fingers in his jeans pocket and crossed them so that no one would be able to see, but he needed his old magic to work now. He needed to know that his dad would be home early tonight and that everything was alright.

"Yes, Mrs. Miller. My Dad does, too. He works in the Twin Towers, in the North Tower, on the 102nd or 103rd floor." Vinny looked as if he were about to cry. Jake really felt sorry for him, but he was feeling even sorrier for himself now. He had a weird feeling deep in his stomach that something really was wrong and that sneakers and pizza was not going to be his only problem. He really wanted to know what was going on out there in the world outside of Franklin Elementary School.

"Jake, Vinny, boys and girls." Once again Mrs. Miller took a very deep breath and looked at them again as if they were the most pathetic group of kids she'd ever seen. "I did tell you all that I knew, and I don't know much more now. But from what I've heard from the other adults in the building and people coming into the building, it may be more serious than we first thought, but I really do think that you need to wait till you get home and discuss this with your parents. We should have some more news after lunch."

This time, it just didn't work. The once budding authors in Mrs. Miller's room were no longer as interested in writing or reading or doing their all-important Social Studies questions as they were before. Once the groups all got together on the floor, they were all talking to each other about what had happened. Jake thought that it was really weird that his teacher didn't even seem to care. Mrs. Miller was very preoccupied with everything else going on as she continually tried her cell phone and the computers. No alien phone calls back to the mother ship, thought Jake and wishing that she was doing just that!

Chapter 9
A Day Like No Other

The day went quickly, it seemed, and before Jake knew it, they were on their way back to the room from lunch. Lunch was uneventful, except for the fact that they weren't able to go out on the playground for recess. They were all told that that was part of the lockdown procedure, whatever that was; because Jake kept thinking that the lockdown wasn't locking out his thoughts today or anybody else's, either. As a matter of fact, more thoughts were dashing through his head today than ever. He wasn't able to eat much of his lunch, which was pretty unusual for him, especially since his Mom had packed a special favorite of his today. He always loved any kind of sandwich she made for him, as long as it was on the special Pita bread that Mrs. Dayman bought in town at their favorite Mid-Eastern restaurant/deli. Mr. Habib, the owner, knew them as regular customers, and when Jake stopped in with his Mom, he always gave Jake a little taste of something special. He'd wink at Jake, and say, "Mmm, deelisius, Jake, no?" Jake usually liked anything that Mr. Habib gave him and found it funny when the man smiled and went through his regular repertoire. But they had been regular customers of the Silk Road Restaurant/Deli for many years, and he knew Mr. Habib for as long as he could remember. He especially loved when Mr. Habib gave him a piece of sesame candy or some Pistachio nuts, and, as always, the Pita bread made the best sandwiches ever. But not today. Today, even the Pita from Mr. Habib didn't seem to taste as good as it usually did.

As the class walked back from lunch, Dylan Hodges started acting like a jerk again.

33

"Hey, did ya' hear? They're coming for us; they're coming right at our school" And he made a noise that sounded like an airplane that he must have learned when he was four years old.

Boy, Jake thought, why did he have to go and act like such a jerk now. Couldn't Dylan act his age just once? Just for today?

That was all poor Vinny needed. Dylan had sent him over the top with his comment. "Shut up, Dylan, just shut up," quivered Vinny.

"Boy," thought Jake to himself. I've never heard Vinny act like that. Poor kid, he must be really nervous. Poor me, too, he thought I'm getting really nervous.

Dylan, however, wasn't about to let Vinny get away with telling him to shut up.

"Are you talking to me, Vinny, Whinny? You can't be." With that, he shoved Vinny.

Jake and Andrew walking next to each other gave each other a look and then glared at Dylan. "Leave him alone, Dylan," said Jake. Don't you care about what's going on?" "Leave him alone."

"You're a real jerk, Dylan," said Andrew.

With that, Dylan went to pull Andrew from the back of his shirt collar, but Jake saw and nudged into Dylan, who let out a "Get off me!"

That, of course, signaled Mrs. Miller to turn around. "What's happening? What is wrong, boys? Turn around and walk appropriately. This is not the day for this nonsense. It's almost time to go home. Get in line, and Dylan, leave Vinny alone!"

That was it? That was all Mrs. Miller was going to do? No detention? No, "I'll call your mother, young man?" Jake thought that this was the strangest day he had ever seen. Everyone was acting strangely. He was happy that there was only a half hour after lunch until they went home. He was happy that he could finally get home and find out what had happened. Maybe Dad would be home earlier than he had planned and he'd find out the news from him, and then they'd go for sneakers and pizza. Jake knew that his Mom and dad were always right up front with him.

When they got back into the classroom, Mrs. Miller said that she needed to talk to them again. Andrew looked at Jake this time, and he seemed to be worried, and Jake was worried and Vinny was on the verge of tears, anyway. Danielle was about to raise her hand, and the whole class looked as if they couldn't wait to hear what their teacher was going to say.

"Children," said Mrs. Miller. "When you go home on the buses, today, get right off at your regular bus stops, and go straight home. Do you understand what I am telling you?"

There it was. Danielle's hand shot straight up in the air. "Mrs. Miller, what is going on? Are we under attack, like some of the other kids are saying? Did the Twin Towers fall? Please, Mrs. Miller." Danielle looked and sounded like she was pleading for her life.

"Danielle," Mrs. Miller took a deep breath, and Jake thought he saw some tears welling up in her eyes, "Children, please just do as we are telling you. Yes, some of this may be true, some may be exaggerated, but this is a very serious matter. Get home safely, go home, and your parents will be able to handle all of this with you. Trust me, trust them. I hope we are all here in school together tomorrow, and then we will be able to make some sense out of this." With that, Mrs. Miller took another deep breath, and her shoulders seemed to fall as she shook her head in what seemed to be disbelief.

That's it, thought Jake. His stomach started to flutter like the whole group of Monarch Butterflies from Third Grade had wound up in his stomach. Right then, right there, he realized that he could finally "read between the lines" as he had learned in Fourth Grade. He knew the difference between "on the lines and in between the lines". He got it, but what he got wasn't what he wanted, and his first thought was, Dad! No, no, he thought, this can't be happening, it just can't be. Magic, magic, cross the fingers, cross them tight, he thought to himself. If I cross them and keep them crossed all the way until I get home, it will work. Dad will be fine, he'll be home when I get there, we'll go to the mall, we will, we will, and then Jake closed his eyes and wished, "Make it be someone else, not my dad." Jake told his mind not to go to that place, what was he thinking? No one said anything about anyone being hurt. Sometimes he thought that if he allowed his mind to think of something bad, it would happen. So, he wasn't going to think about that. He tried as hard as he could to remember the story, he once heard his dad talking about something that had happened at The World Trade Center when Jake was just three years old. Something about a bomb exploding in an underground parking garage. There were many people injured and a few were killed. At least that's what Jake seemed to remember, but he was only three when that happened. Dad doesn't even drive to work, Jake thought, he wouldn't be anywhere near a parking garage. With that thought he took a deep breath and felt like Mrs. Miller. She had been breathing deeply all day, too.

Jake had been so wrapped up in his thoughts that he hadn't even heard what Mrs. Miller was saying, but everyone was getting up, cleaning up packing up and getting ready to go home. There was no homework tonight, no reason to copy the planners. So, he just grabbed his backpack and lined up with the class to go home. Finally!

Chapter 10
The Quiet Before the Storm

Jake and Andrew sat together on the bus ride home. They always felt lucky that they were on the same bus, because sometimes you could live around the corner from your friend, and not be on the same bus route.

It was Andrew who spoke first to Jake. "Days don't worry. My guess is that this is just one big blown-up thing. We'll get the real scoop from our Moms. Who are you listening to? Dylan Hodges or Paul Silver? I really think we'd know more, Mrs. Miller would have told us more, if this thing were really, really bad."

There it was again, thought Jake. This "THING". Why did everyone keep calling it a THING? Even so, he wasn't going to let go of his fingers. It always worked; it would work now.

"I don't know, Sunny, I just don't know. I feel weird about this, like it's really bad. I just don't feel much like talking."

For the rest of the bus ride home, Jake looked out the window and wasn't much aware of the other kids or Andrew on the bus. He just couldn't think of anything else except getting home and finding out what had really happened in the world on September 11th, 2001, Tuesday Pizza and Gym Day.

The streets look okay, Jake thought, but why wouldn't they? This wasn't Manhattan, this was Long Island, this was a car ride or a train ride away from the city., the Big Apple.

Andrew's stop was first and as he got up, he tapped Jake on the shoulder.

"Days, bye. Stop looking so weird, Days. Everything's gonna' be fine. See you tomorrow."

"Bye, Sunny. See you." Jake said without really looking away from the window.

The next stop was Jake's, corner of Boxwood Drive and Wildwood Drive. His house was two from the corner, and he had always been happy that he could really see his house when he got off the bus. When he was younger, it always made him feel really secure to see his house as soon as he got off the bus. What he first noticed was that the Moms of the little kids were at the bus stop as they always were. Only today, as the little kids got off the bus first, their Moms seemed to grab them and hug them, as if they had been away for a month. Jake knew everyone on the block, but by the time he stepped off the bus, everyone was already on their way to their houses. Jake started to sprint towards his house when he noticed it. Mom's car was in the driveway, and so was his Aunt Isabel's. Jake ran right through the side door into the mudroom and then the kitchen.

Chapter 11
Pizza and Worries

The first thing he noticed was that the television was on in the kitchen. Mom didn't usually listen to the television in the afternoon, if she was home at all, and then he realized that his Mom wasn't even supposed to be home. It was supposed to be a late night for her, that's why he, Ben and Dad were going to the mall tonight. Maybe she was just home between her daytime and evening clients. Work, magic, work, Jake said to himself.

As soon as his Mom saw him, she got up from the kitchen table and went to him with a big hug, and began to whimper. She held on to him, and wouldn't let go.

"Oh, Jake, Jake, I'm so sorry, so sorry, everything has changed. I couldn't pick you up at school, honey, I couldn't leave the house, I…" his Mom started to cry softly.

Aunt Isabel got up from her chair, at the kitchen table, too. "Sherry, let him come in and sit down. Please Sherry. Jake, do you know what happened today? What did you learn about this thing in school?" Aunt Isabel had the same look on her face that Mrs. Miller, Mrs. Petrie and all the other adults he had seen today had on their faces. It was really bad, now he knew it for sure!

Ben came down the hall from his room and into the kitchen, too. He just sort of stood there behind Aunt Isabel, looking at Jake and the television playing in the kitchen. It was then that Jake was able to focus on the TV.

The first thing he saw was a replay of the first American Airlines jetliner crashing into the north tower of the World Trade Center, tearing a gaping hole in the building and setting it afire. He couldn't believe what he saw, couldn't even believe that it was happening or had happened. This was not what he had pictured all day in school while the rest of the word was actually knowing and watching. He couldn't believe it, but as the tears welled up in his eyes, and he heard the news commentator.

"The attack began at 8:45 AM when American Airlines Flight 11, a 315,000 pound Boeing 767 carrying 92 people from Boston to Los Angeles crashed into One World Trade Center, apparently several stories above the 80th floor and disappeared into the structure. Meanwhile, huge red and orange fireballs roared higher and higher from a gaping hole in the structure, standing out brightly against the azure sky."

The television's screen switched to the street and someone looking like a petrified character from a horror movie said, "At "first we just saw papers and stuff coming down, but then you noticed that it wasn't just papers, it was people, and they were jumping. This was before the second plane hit."

Jake couldn't take his eyes off the screen, he couldn't understand what he had just seen or heard. The second plane, what second plane? No one had ever said anything about a second plane all day long.

The newswoman continued, "At 9:03 AM, a United Airlines Flight 175, a Boeing 767 carrying 65 people from Boston to Los Angeles, sliced into the midsection of Two World Trade Center. Another grisly shower of debris rained on the streets."

Sherry Dayman walked over to Jake and Ben and held both of their hands, as they continued to watch the screen that now held all the unlocked secrets of truth for Jake.

"Meanwhile, American Airlines Flight 77, A Boeing 757, carrying 58 passengers from Dulles International Airport outside Washington, D.C. to Los Angeles, had turned on a course toward the Pentagon, where 24,000 people work. The jet crashed into the Pentagon at 9:45 am, causing an unknown number of fatalities and dozens of injuries. Part of the building collapsed."

Jake stared frozen-eyed at the television. What were they saying? Did he comprehend? Did he really read between the lines, he thought? Could this be true, or was this some kind of a joke? Jake looked up at his Mom, Aunt Isabel and Ben, and he knew all too well that this was not a joke. This THING, as everyone in school had been calling it all day long, was really true.

"Jake, Jake, listen to me. We heard from Dad. He called this morning. We're still waiting now and we..." Sherry Dayman tried her best to get the words out, but she dropped her shoulders and sobbed quietly.

Aunt Isabel had always been a comforting force in Jake and Ben's life and she was trying to do her best, going from her sister to Jake and Ben, bringing coffee, water, setting out sandwiches for all of them on the table, but it all just seemed like a bad dream to Jake.

Jake looked back at the now dreaded television, and heard, "With all eyes by then on the burning World Trade Center, Tower Two collapsed at 10am, falling straight down, and Tower One disappeared into its own rubble 29 minutes later"

Now the voices on the screen seemed to fade into the distance as the reporter said, "...Flight 93, A Boeing 757 en route from Newark to San Francisco, carrying 38 passengers, five flight attendants and two pilots crashed southeast of Pittsburgh around 10 am. It was believed that this plane might have been headed for the White House, Camp David or the U.S. Capitol building."

The images switched to an inserted photo of Governor George Pataki, Governor of New York, as the reporter said, "Governor George Pataki in calling out the National Guard, called the attack "an attack on our freedom and our way of life. We must retaliate."

"That's it, that's it!" shouted Ben. "I can't listen, anymore, Mom, I can't. It's the same thing over and over again, since I got home. Where's Dad, huh? You keep saying he's all right, then where is he? When you hear from him and they get the Terrorists, let me know, okay. I'll be in my room. Mom, I'm sorry, I just can't listen anymore, Mom. I can't," Ben said as he held back his tears. He hugged Mom and Aunt Isabel as he went back down the hall to his room.

Chapter 12
The Call No One Expected

Jake felt like he had just come back from the land of the living dead as he turned his attention back to his Mom and aunt. He finally got it, he thought, but what was Ben talking about, terrorists?

Jake looked over to them seated at the kitchen table. "Mom, Aunt Isabel, where is Dad? Is he okay? You said you heard from him, where is he? When will he be home, please, Moms, please, tell me. And what's Ben talking about, what terrorists." Jake felt as if he couldn't breathe. He was able to understand what he had heard, although he didn't really want to believe it, and so he resorted to crossing his fingers again, while he waited for one of the adults to answer him.

"Jakie," began Aunt Isabel. Do you understand what you just saw? Do you, sweetie?" She didn't even wait for an answer from Jake. "Your dad called this morning, Jake. He called Mom from his office. He was there, Jake, he was in his office on the 52nd floor, Jake. He called Mom to tell her what had happened, but she had already left for her first client's house, Jake. She didn't talk to him. He left a message on the machine." Aunt Isabel paused. "He got out, Jake, he called again. It was about ten-thirty; he left another message for all of you. He's alright, he's out, and he's trying to get home. The cell phones aren't working properly, it's hard to get to a phone, and the trains were not running. Actually, Manhattan was just shut down, closed off from the rest of the world. But now it seems that they're going to open the trains again, start allowing them to leave the city. The city was just a mass of chaos and confusion, Jake. Everything was emptied, the stock exchange was closed, so was the United Nations, the subways, bridges and tunnels into and out of Manhattan. Businesses closed, and everyone is trying to get away from Manhattan. All of the airports were shut down in New York City since right after the attacks. Now they have been closed down all together, all throughout the United States, the first time in history. Jill Sunshine, Andrew's Mom called to see about your dad. Andrew's dad wasn't in the city today; he was in Atlanta since very early this morning on a business trip and he can't even get home. People are actually walking across the bridges, Jake. But your dad is all right, Sweetie. He's on his way home, we just don't know the way he will get here, but he is. Thank God, Jake, he's on his way home. He's one of the lucky ones." Aunt Isabel came over to him to hug him, as Jake moved away.

He understood why everyone was hugging each other; it was a common ritual in his family. They were always very warm and loving to each other, even the men, and he didn't think anything strange about it, it was just that right now he wanted answers, real answers and he knew Aunt Isabel would tell him, even if Mom was too upset and all the other adults in the world, except the news reporters, were unable to talk about this "THING."

"Aunt Isabel are you sure, about Dad. Are you sure?" Jake realized that his right hand was still in his jeans pocket with his fingers crossed. He wouldn't let go, not until he heard from his dad again or he walked through the door of their house. Right now, he couldn't care less about sneakers or pizza or the mall. Right now, he felt angry and guilty that this morning in school it all seemed so important to him. How could he have been so dumb? He finally understood the gravity of the situation, and all he could think about, and wish for, was that his dad was all right. He never stopped for a Moment to think about anything else. Not yet.

This time it was Mom who answered him. "Jakie, yes, he is. He is all right. What Aunt Isabel told you is the truth, we're not sugarcoating anything for you or Ben or any of us. You know we wouldn't do that,

Jake, we never do. You know that we believe that you and Ben always have the right to know what is going on around you, that we feel that's the only way you can both learn to make good and reasonable decisions and choices. That will never change. Dad is all right, he's safe, and he's trying to get home. I would play the message on the tape for you if I hadn't been so nervous when I got home. I pressed the wrong button and erased both of his messages. We'll hear from him again, soon, sweetie. That's what we told Ben, too. We will. I know we will."

Chapter 13
Doubts and Realities

"Jakie, let me tell you about this morning. Your Mom has gone over it so many times, the phone hasn't stopped ringing, everyone in the world we know has called to find out about your Dad. She's exhausted, Jake. She went to a client's house this morning and did a two-hour workout with her from eight-thirty to ten-thirty. By the time Mom got into her car it was after ten-thirty when she heard the news! She was hysterical and thank God she came right home. I had heard about it while I was watching television this morning and came racing right over here. I was here, thank goodness, when Mom came in. She ran right to the answering machine, I heard the messages with her, but instead of pressing the replay button, she pressed the delete, and the messages from your Dad were gone! But we both heard him, sweetie, as clear as a bell. He was out of the building and safe." Aunt Isabel looked like she had been through a lot, just like Mom did. Just like the whole world had, Jake thought. Just like the whole world, forever changed.

"I just didn't know what was going on," Jake answered. "No one told us too much in school. Mrs. Miller tried to explain to us; she told us more than any of the other teachers did. She was honest with us, I guess, without trying to worry us too much. But we didn't really know that it was an attack," as Jake said the word, the reality of it hit him and he began to shake. He felt his right hand in his pocket, his fingers were starting to hurt, but he couldn't uncross them, he wouldn't. Not until Dad walked through the door, or they heard from him, again.

"All those people, Aunt Isabel, all the people in the buildings. What does all this mean? What do they mean, terrorists? What's going to happen to all of us? Are we safe?" Jake couldn't get the words out fast enough; couldn't possibly comprehend all of the information he had heard in the short time that he had been home.

Sherry Dayman and Isabel Abraham looked over at Jake. They both looked like they couldn't handle anymore questions, but Aunt Isabel spoke first.

"So sad, Jake, so sad. Sadder than anything that any of us have ever lived through before. This is like nothing we have ever seen, Jake. We don't know all of the answers. We don't know most of them. I know it's comforting to think that the adults in your life have all the answers, and sometimes we pretend or think we do. But this time, sweetie, we just don't."

Jake noticed that Ben had emerged from his room. Ben had been crying, and this frightened Jake almost more than anything he had seen or heard today.

"I can't turn the television off, Mom, I've been watching in my room, anyway. They say that warships and aircraft carriers are headed for the New York coast to protect us from further attack and to reduce the number of ships in port. They're also sending guided missile destroyers capable of shooting down aircraft. Mom, Aunt Isabel, uh, Jake, I'm sorry. Sorry I acted the way I did. I guess I'm just so nervous. Nervous and worried and scared. I think we're at war, I think that's what it all means. Does it Mom? Does it Aunt Iz?"

"Oh, Ben," Sherry Dayman looked at her son and shook her head. I don't know how to answer you, I just don't. Like Aunt Isabel said, we adults, don't have the answers. This is a catastrophe, an attack on the world, not just the World Trade Center. We don't have the answers either. Our government officials don't have the answers, but we have to believe. We have to believe that we are safe, that the people in charge know what they are doing, that a huge mistake occurred that allowed this to ever happen and that they have it all under control now. That's what I have to believe for today, at least. That's about all we can do for now. Believe, Jakie, believe, Ben. That's what's going to get us all through this. The belief that we are Americans, that this is the Land of the Free and the Home of the Brave. No, we never, ever have experienced anything like this before. Aunt Isabel and I remember when we were even younger than you are now, Jake. We were in First Grade, not in the same class; they didn't ever keep twins in the same classes, back then. But we were in First Grade, unable to understand too much at all, but we'll never forget it…the day that President Kennedy was shot. Everyone talked about it forever, mourned him forever. This is a day like that one, boys,," and Mrs. Dayman paused. "Only worse, boys, much worse. Yes, I think we will retaliate, that's what President Bush said. It will be a war, but one that is different from any other that America has seen."

"I think the best thing we can do is eat these sandwiches because we have to keep up our energy," said Aunt Isabel, "stay close to each other right here in the kitchen, watch the television, keep the phone lines open, as we are doing, and pray. Pray that all will be right with the world after today, although it may be changed forever. And we'll pray that your dad comes home very soon, and we'll pray for everyone else in the world and all of those poor lost souls who lost their lives today. And for the hope of finding most of the people alive, God only knows what is in the rubble." Aunt Isabel stopped.

No one said a word, but they all understood that there really was nothing to say anymore. Nothing to do, nothing to say. Aunt Isabel told them that her husband, Uncle Greg, had already gone down to the local hospital to donate blood. He had called her on her cell phone to tell her that there were so many people in line waiting to give blood that the Blood Bank had been turning them away, thanking them, and telling them that they had more blood now than they could use. No one was even sure if there were enough survivors to need the blood, he said.

Chapter 14
A Teacher's Secret

They ate the sandwiches, and Jake had to admit to himself that he was really pretty hungry. Starving. He had been unable to eat his favorite lunch at school and now it was almost five thirty. He hadn't realized that so much time had passed. He figured that Aunt Isabel had brought over the sandwich stuff or bought them, because his Mom didn't usually make this kind of food. Roast beef, and corned beef, all of his dad's favorites, and two big bags of potato chips, and not the baked kind, either, the regular kind. As he was devouring the sandwich, Jake thought to himself that he was supposed to be enjoying pizza at the mall with his dad, and felt sorry that he had worried so much about his dad getting home tonight on time to take him out for pizza and his sneakers. He'd give anything now to just have his dad home with them. Wow, he thought, that seemed like a lifetime ago when he had those thoughts, a lifetime ago, before the world was forever changed.

It wasn't easy eating the sandwich with his fingers crossed, but Jake didn't care, and no one seemed to notice him, either, they were all wrapped up in their thoughts of despair and disbelief. Just then they all looked up at the television screen again as they heard the voice of New York City's beloved Mayor Rudolph Giuliani. Jake had often heard his parents, their friends and his relatives talking about Rudy Giuliani as the savior of New York City. They all loved him because they said he had actually cleaned up New York City and made it such a great place to live, work and to visit. Whenever his parents would take him into the city for something special, a museum or a sporting event or such, they always

49

mentioned the mayor. When Jake saw him on the news, it brought him a sense of relief, as if he was an old family friend there to report to Jake. The mayor was urging New Yorkers to stay home and not try to get down to the area south of Canal Street. He said that the area was, in fact, evacuated. When asked about the number of people killed, Giuliani replied, "I don't think we want to speculate about that more than any of us can bear." Then, the mayor urged New Yorkers to stay home on Wednesday. Jake thought that Mayor Giuliani looked sadder than anyone he had seen today, if that was possible.

And on and on the news went. When the phone rang, Aunt Isabel answered. She told everyone who called the same thing: "Marc is all right. Yes, yes, he's on his way home. Thank you, no there's nothing you can do. Yes, I'll tell Sherry." And then Jake's attention would turn back to the news and Ben and his Mom.

For the next few hours, that's all there was, nothing more. Sometimes Jake felt like he could hardly keep his head up, hardly keep his eyes open, but he was afraid to fall asleep, afraid that he couldn't keep his fingers crossed while he slept, either.

So it was back to the nightmare of the television screen which told the rest of the horror. The other buildings around the World Trade Center were on fire, Building 7 had collapsed, and others remained ablaze. U.S. officials were reporting that there were good indications that Saudi militant Osama bin Laden, the same man who was suspected of coordinating the bombings of two U.S. Embassies in 1998 was involved in the attacks today.

"Oh my God, my God, said Sherry Dayman. I've read about him, heard about him before. Isabel, do you remember anything about him?"

"I think I do, Sherry, I heard something when we were in college about him. But that was a long time ago, I'm not sure."

The phone rang, and they all felt as if they were jumping out of their skin every time the phone rang. Jake heard Aunt Isabel say "Hi,

Andrew," but he wasn't sure. He had been so caught up in his own thoughts, worries and fears, he never even thought about Andrew or his dad in Atlanta.

"Let me see, Andrew, we're keeping the phone line open, so we're not staying on the phones, dear. I'll ask Jake, and he'll call you back, he can use my cell phone." Aunt Isabel put the phone down on the receiver again.

"Jakie, Andrew wanted to know if you were okay. He wanted to know if he should come over."

Jake thought for a Moment. He always wanted to be with Sunny, but right now he just couldn't. He felt as if he had to concentrate only on Dad, the finger crossing magic and getting Dad home.

"No, Aunt Isabel, I don't think so, not now, I just can't. Can I use your cell phone to call him? I would like to talk to him for just a minute."

"Here, sweetie. Maybe talking to Sunny will make you feel better. Take your mind off everything for a few minutes. It won't hurt, it's okay to relax a little, I promise you."

"Thanks, Aunt Iz; I'll only be a minute."

Jake took the phone into the den and punched in Andrew's phone number. He was getting pretty good at doing things one-handed, and he smiled to himself, if just for an instant. Mrs. Sunshine answered the phone on the first ring.

"Mrs. Sunshine, it's Jake. Can I please speak to Andrew? Oh, Mrs. Sunshine, How's Mr. Sunshine? My Mom and Aunt told me about his being in Atlanta."

"Hi Jake, dear. Thanks for asking. He's just fine, stuck in his hotel, but safe. I guess. I don't know if any of us are safe, now, are we? I'll get Andrew for you; he's been waiting to hear from you, dear."

Jake thought that Mrs. Sunshine had sounded very different. She was nice and kind as she always was, but he knew that everyone and everything had changed forever, and he was beginning to realize that no matter what, everyone and everything they all knew had changed on some level.

"Days, I'm glad you called me back, I wasn't sure if you would. I guess you were the one who was right about all of this. My Dad wasn't even there, in the city I mean, I forgot he went on a business trip. But your dad, he's uh, on his way home, I hear. You thought you sounded lame in school, but you were right. Now I feel lame. Can you believe it, Days? Can you?"

"No, Sunny, I can't. I'm waiting to hear from my dad again. He's on his way home. But we aren't sure how. But the important thing is that he made it out. He made it out. And I heard about your dad, and he's okay, too. I guess we're pretty lucky. They think there's going to be a war, Sunny. A war! We've never been in a war before. It all seems like that end of the world movie we rented, remember?"

"Yeah, I was thinking that, too, when I was watching the TV. My Mom keeps telling me that it will all be all right. But even though she never lies to me, somehow, it's really hard to believe."

Jake couldn't seem to talk any longer, so he told Andrew that he was really tired and that he had to get off the phone.

"Okay, Days, I'll see you in school tomorrow. Everyone's saying we'll have school. My Mom says that the city schools will probably close, but we will have school. I think President Bush said so. See ya' tomorrow. And Days don't worry. I know I told you that all day, but your dad will be home."

Jake walked back into the kitchen and gave the phone to his aunt. The kitchen clock said that it was seven o'clock. There really wasn't a sound in the house now, except for the television. Aunt Isabel was cleaning up the table and had convinced her sister to lie down in the den on the couch. Jake thought that there just wasn't much else to say, so he went into the den to be with his Mom and Ben. If it had been a winter night, he would have felt like asking his Mom for a fire in the fire-place to warm them up while they snuggled under Grandma's big crocheted blanket, but it was like a hot summer's night and Jake knew really that the cold was only coming in from their hearts, not the weather.

Chapter 15
Rumors and The Unknown

The anchorwoman on the news said that there would be an Address to the Nation from President Bush at 8:30, and Sherry Dayman said that she was anxious to hear what he would say. Just as she finished her sentence, Jake heard something, and he knew it was the garage door opening. Dad! It was Dad! He looked at his Mom and Ben and before they knew it, they were all up running into the kitchen as Dad walked through the door.

"Marc, Oh, Marc!" Mom raced to him, as he came forward to embrace all three of them, as Aunt Isabel joined in the group hug.

Jake thought he had never felt a hug like this before, never felt so warm and wonderful all at once. Still sad, but seeing his father made everything seem better, and he realized that his fingers were hurting as he pried them apart.

He had never seen his dad look the way he did now. None of them were prepared for what they saw. Dad's eyes were brimming with tears, as he said, "I knew I'd see you again. I knew I would. I believed it with all of my heart, and I got here."

Dad was completely disheveled. His suit was crumpled and covered in whitish soot. His face showed all of the signs of the day.

"Aunt Isabel was the first to talk. "Marc, sit down, you look like you can't stand anymore. Are you hungry, thirsty? What can I do for you?"

Dad just shook his head no. "Nothing, not now, Isabel, not now."

Chapter 16
Questions Without Answers

Mom helped Dad out of his clothes and into the shower. Jake had noticed that Dad just smelled all over like a burning fire, but no one mentioned it. The smell seemed to linger throughout the house as a reminder of where Marc Dayman had been and what he had been through. He and Ben stayed in the den with Aunt Isabel, who kept calling Uncle Greg on his cell phone to find out that he was now on his way over to their house, too.

Later on, in the evening, when Dad was able to come out of the bedroom, showered and cleaned up he sat with all of them in the den for a while. He wanted to talk; he wanted to tell them about what had happened, about the way he got home by walking to Penn Station through the crowds and the people running, about the attack and what he saw, the horror of it, the senselessness of the deaths. Some of it, Jake knew he was trying not to say in front of him and Ben, but he did explain a lot of it, or what he could tonight.

"The building actually shook. That giant building, it shook," Dad said in a hushed tone. "And I called you, Sherry. That's when I called. But I knew that we had to get out, even though they were telling us on the bullhorns to remain calm, stay where we were, not to panic. But we were all in full-fledged panic! Some of us just raced for the stairs. We just raced down. It was surreal, it didn't seem as though it could have been happening, at all. As we raced down, we saw the firemen racing up the stairs! They were racing up into a burning tower!! Every fireman I saw is probably dead! Many of them were the people who helped us to get away from the building. They are all heroes, so, so many of them! What else can I say? What can I say?"

Dad shook his head and buried his face in his hands. Jake didn't think he had ever seen his dad cry before. It hurt him.

"But I'm here," Marc Dayman continued. "I'm here, and I'll be all right."

The night continued and Aunt Isabel and Uncle Greg stayed with the Daymans until they were certain that everyone would be okay. They watched President Bush's address and heard what he had to say. They discussed the fact that none of them had voted for George Bush, but they were pretty impressed with what he had to say tonight. Jake, though half asleep on the couch, felt some comfort in knowing that his family felt secure about their President and that he was going to be doing the right things to protect them and their country. He said that "thousands of lives were suddenly ended by evil," and asked for the families and victims, but also said "that these acts shattered prayers for steel, but they cannot dent the steel of American resolve." He also said that we as Americans would have to go on with our lives and show the terrorists that they cannot stop us.

"Jake, Ben, come on, let's get you guys to bed. Tomorrow is a school day. You heard what the President said. We go on with our lives. You go to school. We have to show them." Marc Dayman forced himself up from the couch to help Jake and Ben to their rooms as if doing what he did every other night was of extreme importance to him.

Jake drifted off to sleep thinking about the day and his fears and the question in his mind, "Who is the "them" that I keep hearing everyone talk about?"

Chapter 17
The Unseen Crisis

Wednesday morning came and the alarm clocks in the Dayman household went off, just as they always did. Jake sensed a feeling of heaviness, but he kept reminding himself that this was to be forever now. He knew what the President meant, they all had to do their jobs, go to work, go to school and be the best they could be. Dad and Mom were discussing it as the news channel played in the background constantly on the Television. Mom was saying how it seemed so odd to not hear any airplanes passing overhead. Jake kept thinking how very different and yet the same that everything felt to him. The newspaper on the kitchen counter had headlines and pictures to prove that yesterday's events had not been a dream!

"Boys, Dad is going to go to his office on Long Island, today, to see what he can work out there until the offices are moved somewhere else. He's going to be leaving later than usual, so he thought it might be a treat to drop you both off at school this morning. That will give you a few more minutes."

When they finished their breakfast, they got into Dad's SUV, headed for Ben's school first. Dad made the turn into "town," and said, "I'm going to stop at Mr. Habib's for a cup of coffee. Want anything, guys?"

"Yeah, sure," they both said, almost in unison. A snack for school today would be great, Jake thought. Maybe some white pistachios, one of his favorites. Anything to help wash away yesterday, he thought.

Dad parked right outside the deli, and they all walked in. They were pretty lucky today, Mr. Habib wasn't crowded, as a matter of fact, there was only one other customer in the store. Mr. Habib was just finishing up with the man buying coffee, when they walked in.

"Good morning," Marc Dayman said. I'll have a coffee, and the boys are choosing something to take along. How are you, Mr. Habib?"

Mr. Habib never looked up from the coffee. He never looked at Marc Dayman or Ben or Jake. Jake thought it was very odd, in fact, it was the first time ever that Mr. Habib had not offered a taste of this or that for Jake or Ben or even smiled at them. Jake and Ben put their snacks on the counter. When their dad took out his money to hand it to Mr. Habib, he just shook his head without ever looking up and said, "No charge, today. No charge. Just take it. My gift. I am American, too, and I am sorry."

Jake didn't know what was going on, but his dad put his money away and just said, "Thank you, Mr. Habib. I hope you have a good day. I understand. Come, boys."

As Jake got into the truck, he looked back at the window of Mr. Habib's store and sadly read the sign, "Silk Road Restaurant/Deli." "The First Day you Meet you are Friends. The next Day you meet, you are Brothers." Established 1986.

"Dad, what was that all about, what's up with Mr. Habib?" asked Ben.

"Yeah, he's always been so nice and so friendly to us. I don't get it, either," said Jake. "Maybe he lost someone or something has happened to someone he knew. I hope not." Jake said.

Boys," replied Marc Dayman. Everyone is going to know someone, somewhere, who has lost their life in this tragedy. Everyone will be touched by this thing, and everything will be forever changed. I don't know what happened to Mr. Habib, but I have a good idea. We'll talk about it later."

Chapter 18
Coming to Terms

Jake was happy to be in school today, happy to be in his schedule where things always seemed secure. Yesterday had been such a strange and awful day that he felt today would just put everything into perspective.

Most of his class was in school, but some of the kids had stayed home. Mrs. Miller had discussed their absences because she knew that everyone would be curious. Four children were absent, she had said, Vinny Carroll, Kazzim Buhkiar, Sarah Flynn, and David Karr. Sarah and David had both gone home early on Tuesday, and Mrs. Miller said that they might have been sick or had a specific reason for staying home. She wasn't sure about Kazzim, although he wasn't ever absent, and Vinny Carrol's family had suffered a huge loss. And that's all she said, and it was time for Jake to go down for the pledge.

Every morning the school would stand for the Pledge of Allegiance, led by the Student Council over the loudspeaker. Jake was Co-President of the Student Council, with Andrew, and this morning, as every Wednesday, was his turn to lead the school in the Pledge. When he went into the office, Dr. Snow told him that there would be a Moment of silence after the Pledge and that today, of all days, the Pledge would be more important than ever. She said to make sure to say it slowly, to allow everyone to think about the words of freedom and what they actually meant. Jake understood what she was saying to him and did just that. He felt proud of himself, saddened, but proud to be an American.

When he got back to class, Mrs. Miller said that they would, once again, discuss yesterday's tragedy. Jake thought to himself that the "THING" had now turned into a tragedy. She explained that she had hoped she had done the "right "thing for them all yesterday, and they talked openly about the attack and what it meant to them as young people in America and in New York. She told them how lucky she felt, because both of her sons and her daughter-in-law were safe, and that her cousin who worked at Windows on the World, had been late for a meeting, gotten off the subway, and seen the building ablaze! She said that there were so many stories like hers, and yet so many that were so different and so unfortunate.

Danielle raised her hand, and Jake had a feeling that she would definitely have something of urgency to say. They hadn't had any homework last night, and it surely couldn't be her usual questions about that.

"Mrs. Miller," Danielle began. She already sounded like she had run the marathon, Jake thought. "Mrs. Miller, I have some very sad news to report," ...and Danielle took a breath... "About Vinny Carroll. Actually, about his..."

"Yes, Danielle, I know. I was just about to tell all of you. Vinny's father worked at the World Trade Center, I believe in the same tower as your father, from what I heard, Jake, but...um, he was on one of the top floors, one of the companies that had no chance of um, ah, getting out. Children, Vinny's dad has not been found." Mrs. Miller looked as if she would cry, and a silence fell over the class.

Mrs. Miller continued sadly, "Boys and girls, I thought about this all night, as soon as I got the phone call at home from Dr. Snow. We will all have to pitch in and help each other, especially Vinny; he will need all of us, when he returns to school. One of the best ways that I know of to express our feelings and help us all through this is to write. I thought we would work on a book, a special book, throughout the year. You can each do whatever you'd like. Letters, essays, poems, stories, remembrances, research, whatever you'd like. I'll help you, we'll help each other, and it will be good for us. We can even dedicate it to Vinny's father, if you'd like, and have it as something special for him. I also had another thought, you can tell I didn't sleep much last night, but I thought that we should make something patriotic. Perhaps you'd like to work in your groups to come up with some ideas, come to a consensus on what you'd like to do."

As the class moved into their groups, many had ideas to share. Some of the kids just wanted to talk about what had happened, about what was happening, before thinking about their class book and patriotic project. Mrs. Miller had talked about patriotism, and of course all of the children had heard on television and the news about showing what it meant to be American. Flags seemed to be a natural idea for the class.

Jake had thought that it was odd in a way to be thinking about being patriotic now when the world seemed to be falling apart. He looked around the class at his friends and teacher and couldn't help but think of the changes that had occurred to all of their lives. And he thought of Vinny and the changes that were in store for him. Jake felt a pang of guilt when he remembered how he had wished and prayed that it would happen to someone else in his class or someone else he knew, but not him, not his dad! Now here he was making flags with his group and talking about patriotism. Vinny was home with his family hoping that his father would be found. He knew that in some small way the flags and pins of American flags and signs that were already going up in everyone's door and cars would not really beat the enemy, but it would help them to feel better. It was a good feeling to come together like this and he was happy that Mrs. Miller was letting them work on something to help their feelings.

Mrs. Petrie, the teacher next door, came in to see what Mrs. Miller's class was doing. She looked around while Mrs. Miller told her about the flags. The class had decided to make American flags. Everyone would make one to bring home for their doors and each group would make an extra for the students who weren't in class on Wednesday. They had even decided to sign each of their names on the white stripes of the flags and make an extra-large one for the door of Room One, their classroom door.

Everyone was very busy working on the flags. Jake noticed that for once even Dylan Hodges seemed to be serious about what he was doing and concentrating on their project. Maybe part of being patriotic, Jake thought, was all pulling together and working as one. Even though they all really felt very insecure about their lives and about the War that President Bush had promised, Jake felt a certain sense of security here in school working together with his classmates and doing something to help.

"We need as many markers and scissors as we can get together, people," said Mrs. Miller. "If you have any in your book bags, please get them and share them with your groups. You're working so nicely, thank you, children. I knew you were the best class I've ever had." Mrs. Miller smiled that same smile that she had used the day before, on Tuesday, the day when everyone was acting so strangely and the day when everything changed forever. But today Jake knew what Mrs. Miller was feeling and why.

Jake and the rest of his group got up to go to their book bags. He realized that this was probably the first day in Fifth Grade that they hadn't started the day with their Math Problem of the Day. Yes, everything was so different. As Jake opened his book bag, he looked in and realized that it wasn't his book bag at all! None of the supplies were his, and as he pulled out one of the notebooks to check, he read the name Kazzim Buhkiar. He must have taken Kazzim's book bag instead of his own yesterday when they were packing up to go home! Kazzim probably had his book bag. He looked at the identification label on the bag and noticed the address, 246 Broad Street. Jake thought for sure that it was an address right in the middle of town. He didn't know anyone who lived in the middle of town.

Jake walked over to the front of the room where Mrs. Miller was talking to one of the groups on the floor. "Mrs. Miller, excuse me, but I just looked in my book bag and I have Kazzim's instead of mine. I guess he has mine. Maybe I can call him after school and get it if he does. My Mom will probably take me over to his house, if she knows where it is."

"That's very kind of you, Jake. Kazzim lives with his aunt and uncle above their restaurant in town. The Silk Road Deli/Restaurant. Do you know where it is? It's Middle Eastern food."

"Of course I do," said Jake. "My family has been going there forever; we love their food. We've known Mr. Habib for a long, time. My dad and brother and I stopped there this morning. I'm sure my Mom can take me there after school." Jake thought for a Moment about going on and telling Mrs. Miller about the way that Mr. Habib had acted this morning, but he changed his mind. He was happy that he could go there after school, and he kept thinking how strange it was that he never knew about the connection between Kazzim and Mr. Habib. Jake walked back over to his group to work on the flags.

"We'll get him; we'll get that Osama and all those people. My dad said they should send them all back. We're American and we're gonna' get them," Dylan Hodges boasted to his group.

Andrew was in Dylan's group, unlucky for him! Jake knew that Mrs. Miller had a plan to the groups, and she had evened them out so that they could all work their best together. Kazzim had been placed in the group with Jake since Mrs. Miller knew that Jake had been a "mentor "to him last year in Fourth Grade. Jake realized then that he really didn't know anything personal about Kazzim at all, probably because it was so difficult to really speak to each other.

Dylan, however, wasn't ready to end his tirade. "My dad read the paper to me this morning, it said that Osama guy is the one responsible for the attack and we're going to get him, all of them."

"Dylan," said Mrs. Miller as she walked over to him. "Yes, your dad is correct. And the paper, I assume, is correct. And we can all feel angry and frightened. But we can't turn that fear into hate. Not in my classroom, dear. Do you understand?"

Dylan shook his head yes at Mrs. Miller and looked somewhat embarrassed. That was a first, thought Jake. Dylan feeling embarrassed. But as he thought about Dylan, he began to think about Kazzim and Mr. Habib and thought he just might know why Kazzim wasn't in school today. It must have had something to do with the way Mr. Habib had acted this morning in his store. That's what his dad meant when he said, "I understand."

The class continued to work on their flags and Mrs. Miller knew that they were talking about the attack, about what they heard at home and on the news and about the way they felt. She said that they would get a chance to discuss as much as they wanted, together, later on.

"The problem with this terrible and horrible day, "said Mrs. Miller, "is that none of us really knows what is going to happen or where this may all lead. What we do know is that we are American, we must be proud, we must do what we can to help those who lost loved ones and friends, whether we know them or not. We must do just what President Bush said, we must continue to come to school, to work, go about our jobs and our lives, and not let them get to us. The terrorists must not succeed."

"But they have, Mrs. Miller," said Danielle. "They have. Even if we do all those things that the President says, there is no Twin Towers, most of the people have been killed and we're going to have a war, Mrs. Miller. Even my uncle, the air traffic controller says he doesn't know how this could have happened. How could it?" Danielle looked as if she was going to break down and cry right then and there.

Andrew raised his hand, "That's just it, Danielle, no one does know. My dad is stuck on a business trip in Atlanta; we're all scared stiff, but just think that the people in charge wouldn't let anything really bad happen again." Andrew took a breath. "At least, that's the way I feel, and I believe it. That's why we are making flags and writing a book and that's why we are all putting flags in our cars and houses and giving blood, and all the stuff being done to help everyone. That's what we have to do." Andrew had sounded like he just spilled out everything he knew or had heard in the past day.

"I agree with you, Andrew. We all are a bit frightened and a lot saddened, and we don't know how to handle this because we never have before. But we must believe that we'll get through it. Now, finish your flags, so everyone can put their signatures on and take them home today." Mrs. Miller tried to console them.

Jake was just finishing his job of making sure that everyone in the class signed each flag and thinking that they looked pretty cool when the classroom phone rang. He felt a wave of fear curl through his stomach as the phone monitor told Mrs. Miller that it was for her. He looked around and realized that every other kid in the class was watching Mrs. Miller and the now feared telephone. Was it going to be this way forever, he thought? Were they always going to be afraid of every telephone ring? Would something happen again?

Mrs. Miller got off the phone and looked okay. She noticed the way the students were feeling, it seemed, because she smiled and said, "Children, don't worry. We can't worry each time the phone rings. It was just the school office with some news about schedules, that's all," Mrs. Miller looked around, and sighed, "we're okay, we're all okay."

Chapter 19
A Changed World

Sitting on the bus at the end of the day, September 12th, Jake realized how different it felt from yesterday. Today he was able to talk to Andrew, however.

"Sunny, I'm going to ask my Mom to bring me over to Kazzim's, or, Mr. Habib's store to switch our book bags. Do you want to see if you can come?"

"I don't know, Days; I think I'd better go home and see what's happening. My Mom is still pretty upset about my dad being stuck in Atlanta and no planes flying. It's weird, isn't it?"

"What's weird?' Jake looked over at Andrew.

"The no- noise. We always hear the planes when they change the flight pattern and it seems so quiet." Andrew answered.

"Yes, my Mom mentioned it, too. But everything's weird, Sunny. Everything."

When Jake got home his Mom and Ben were both there. For a few short Moments Jake expected something to be wrong like it was yesterday and he walked into his house half holding his breath. The television was still on continually reporting the news coverage of yesterday's tragedy. Sherry Dayman was on the telephone. Jake felt that pang of butterflies inside his stomach again. He wondered would he get panicky every time he saw his Mom or Mrs. Miller on the phone.

"Mom, I understand completely, and I agree with you. Mom, yes, I do. There's nothing else we can all do. We'll miss you, too, and I know the boys will be so disappointed, but they're old enough to understand. Yes, uh, huh." Jake's Mom paused as she saw him come through the door. "Mom, Jake just came in, I'll talk to you tomorrow, Love you, too. Bye." Sherry Dayman hung up the phone.

"Hi sweetie, how was school?" Jake's Mom had cancelled her clients for a few days and was home. Mr. Dayman was still at his office on Long Island trying to help out there. Just getting people settled and manning the phones, working on all the paperwork and details for the people who were missing was going to be a full-time job for the survivors, for now.

"Was that Grandma on the phone," Jake asked.

"Yes, it was. We were talking about Grandma and Grandpa coming here next week for the holidays, for Rosh Hashanah. You know Jake they're saying that planes will not be flying for a few days and Grandma and Grandpa were coming on Sunday morning, but it just doesn't seem possible or safe right now." Jake's Mom looked at him waiting for him to say something.

She continued. "It was a big decision for us to make, Jake, to not be together for the holidays, but we all felt it would be better for this year. If it were a few weeks later and more of the world was settled and we knew," Sherry Dayman paused, "but not this year. We'll miss them terribly, but I wouldn't feel right about having them take the chance of flying with so much going on."

Jake felt completely disappointed, "I understand, Mom, but it will seem so weird not having Grandma and Grandpa with us for the Jewish Holidays. Why did this all have to happen, why Mom, why?"

Jake knew if he let himself, he would be crying again in an instant, but he just wouldn't let it happen. He had never thought about the ways that the attack would affect his family. He thought that his dad being safe was all they had to fear, but not here it was, this "THING" coming out again, changing things. Would it ever stop?

Ben heard them and came out of his room with his Spanish book in his hand." Que Pasa? What's up? What's going on, hi Jake, boy?" What's wrong, Mom?"

"I just spoke to Grandma and Grandpa, and they won't be coming to New York for the Jewish Holidays, not with everything going on. We decided together that it's not the right time. Not this year."

Ben banged his Spanish book down on the kitchen table, "You know, this just stinks! It just stinks! I agree with your decision, Mom, and you're right, but it just stinks."

"It does, Ben. It more than stinks. But we'll have to make the best of it. Think about how lucky we are and think about those who are so much less fortunate than we are this year. We have to thank God for our blessings, for Dad, for each other and for the strength to help the others. And Ben and Jake, you have a right to be angry, you do. But let's keep it in perspective.

Jake knew his Mom was right. He just didn't want it to be this way; he wanted everything to be the way it was when his only worry was his new cool sneakers and pizza with Dad. That's what he wanted. He just wanted things to be the way they had been. He wanted to go back to his perfect, carefree world.

"So, what was school like today? Did you talk a lot about yesterday, Jake?" Sherry Dayman wanted to move the conversation away from her parents' visit to New York.

"Okay, Mom. We made flags and everyone signed them and we're going to write a book, about the day, about yesterday." But there's some awful news, Mom, about Vinny Carroll's dad."

"Oh, Jakie, I know. I got a phone call about him. You know I knew Mr. Carroll when I worked at the World Trade Center. It's so heartbreaking."

Mrs. Dayman went over to Jake and hugged him tightly as if she was afraid he was going to cry. "We have to thank God every day, Jake, that Dad is all right. That he is a survivor. But we have to help all the others as much as we can. I'm going into the city tomorrow with some other women to help out at the soup kitchens that were set up for all the people working down at Ground Zero. It's a way that I can help at least. Oh, by the way, Jake, Dad called from the Long Island office. He's going to help in setting up an office in a hotel in the city until they know what they're going to do or where they'll go. But that won't start till maybe next week. In the meantime, Dad said to tell you and Ben that he's going to be manning a booth at the mall collecting money for the World Trade Center Relief Fund on the weekend, and he wanted to know if you'd like to come with him and buy your sneakers then."

Jake thought about it for a minute, thought about what his Mom had said about being thankful and blessed. He thought about his fingers being crossed in his pocket for almost the whole day yesterday and he thought about Vinny Carroll and his family.

"Mom, I'd like to go with Dad. Maybe Sunny could come along with us, too. That would be really cool. But Mom, I don't really need the sneakers, but some other kids might. I'd rather have Dad donate the money he would spend on my sneakers to the Relief Fund. Do you think he would?" Jake knew he had made the right decision immediately.

"Jakie, not only will Dad do it, I think you'll make him very proud. And Jake, it would be a wonderful way to begin the New Year."

"Mom, I forgot, for a minute. Kazzim, you know the kid in my class, well he wasn't in school today and I took his book bag yesterday, instead of mine, and I said I'd bring it to him after school, 'cause I didn't think you'd mind. And guess what? Kazzim is Mr. Habib's nephew, and he lives with him right on Broad Street, right above the restaurant. Did you know that, Mom?"

"No, sweetie, I didn't know that. But yes, we can go over there to Mr. Habib's."

"Mom, this morning Mr. Habib was acting really strange. Weird! He wouldn't let Dad pay for his coffee or our stuff and he really didn't even look at us, or talk to us. He told Dad to just take the things that it was a gift or something, because he was American. I don't get what went on, Mom."

Mrs. Dayman shook her head and said, "Jake, this is going to be so difficult on so many levels. Mr. Habib is from Afghanistan. He has been in America for many years, and he has become an American citizen. But people are angry and fearful of anyone from the Middle East, now. People don't know what to do, and when that happens, they become afraid. I understand that too. People start to think that everyone from there is a terrorist. Of course, that is not true, but people are devastated, Jake. So, Mr. Habib probably feels ashamed, embarrassed, saddened by what has happened. I'm sure it is very hard for him and his wife and now that you tell me about Kazzim, he must be worried and concerned about him, as well."

Jake had thought that might be it, but he hadn't been sure. "Mom, I also made a flag for Kazzim since he wasn't in school today. Do you think he'll be happy to get it?"

"Yes, sweetie, I do. Come on, we'll go. Let me just tell Ben... Sherry Dayman turned around to look at Jake for a Moment, "What did I do to deserve a kid like you?"

As they drove through town Jake and his Mom noticed that every store, every house, every car had an American flag on it. Some were plain, some said, "These Colors Don't Run," and some had other Patriotic sayings on them. Both Jake and his Mom couldn't help but notice them all and Jake was happy that his Mom had already put one up on their house. She was going to put the one Jake made in school on their house, too. It made him feel proud to be an American, and if all the flags and acts of patriotism could have washed away the terror, then there were certainly enough to do that, Jake thought.

When they arrived at Mr. Habib's restaurant, Mrs. Dayman was able to find a parking spot right in front of the store, just like yesterday with his dad. Jake noticed that the restaurant was empty again, and no one was at the counter as they walked in. But right on the front of the window of the store was a giant American flag. Jake had the book bag and the flag in his hands.

Mr. Habib came out from the back of the restaurant. He still looked sad and never looked up at them, although he greeted them in a formal sort of way.

"How are you, Mr. Habib?" Mrs. Dayman smiled at him. "How are you and your family doing?"

"We are all right. We are American, you know." Mr. Habib looked so sad as he waved his hand through his restaurant. "I am empty all day. "And then as if he didn't want to say anymore, Mr. Habib said. "How can I help you?"

"Mr. Habib, Kazzim, your nephew, is in my class in school. We switched our book bags yesterday, in our rush, and now I have his and I think Kazzim has mine. So, we brought it over to him." Jake hoped that Mr. Habib was going to respond to him and not turn away as he had been doing. "We also made American flags in school and since Kazzim was absent, I made one for him. We all signed them, see." Jake held the flag up for Mr. Habib to see.

"Thank you, thank you very much, Jake and Mrs. Dayman. Thank you." Mr. Habib looked up at them for the first time. "Kazzim did not attend school today because I was afraid to send him. I was afraid of what the other children would think of him. I was afraid of what they would say to him." Mr. Habib looked up at Jake, and although he didn't smile, he had a gleam of happiness on his face. "But you, Jake, you are a good friend. I think you will make Kazzim very happy. I will get him."

Mr. Habib went to the phone and called Kazzim. Jake guessed that the phone rang upstairs in their apartment over their store, because Kazzim came in from the back of the restaurant, rather quickly. When Kazzim saw Jake he looked surprised to see him. Jake greeted him and gave him his book bag. Kazzim shook his head and smiled, so that Jake knew he realized about the switch of the book bags. Kazzim said something to his uncle that Jake and his Mom could not understand.

"No, Kazzim, I told you, you are American, we are American, and you speak to me in English. Yes, go get Jake's book bag and hurry."

Kazzim was back in a minute and gave Jake his book bag. "Thank you, Jake," he said.

"You're welcome; I also have an American flag for you, Kazzim. We made them today, we all signed them, and you have to put your signature on the last white line, too. We left a space for you. Go ahead, sign it, Kazzim."

Kazzim looked up at his uncle, with a questioning look on his face. "Go ahead, Kazzim, go ahead, my nephew. Sign the flag, here, here is a pen for you. You see, you are an American, too. This proves it." With that, Jake thought he saw a hint of a smile across Mr. Habib's face for the first time today.

As Kazzim signed the flag, Mrs. Dayman said, "Mr. Habib, please forgive me if you think that I am speaking out of turn, but it really might be a good idea if you send Kazzim to school tomorrow. He will be okay in school. It might be better for him."

"Let's put our special flag up first. Then I will think about what is best. Kazzzim, where do you think is the best place for your special flag? Where should we hang it?"

Kazzim looked around and thought for a Moment. "At the front door of the restaurant, Uncle. At the front door is a good place?"

Jake and his Mom smiled. "Yes, Kazzim, "said Mrs. Dayman, if it's okay with your uncle, the front door would be an excellent place to hang the flag."

Now Jake was sure that he saw a big smile spread across Mr. Habib's face, "Yes Kazzim, the front door is a place of honor. A perfect, best place for your special flag from all of your American friends in your class. We will hang it there with your name on the American flag."

With that Mr. Habib taped the flag to the inside of the door facing out. "Come, Kazzim, come Jake, let us look at our beautiful flag. You see, right next to our sign."

Jake and Kazzim and his Mom all went right outside of the door with Mr. Habib to look at the flag

Jake looked around and thought that this was like a movie he had once seen. A much better one than the movie he kept thinking about yesterday. This one was a happy one with a happy ending.

"Look Jake, look Kazzim," said Mr. Habib. You see what the sign says? "The First Day you Meet you are Friends. The next Day you Meet you are Brothers." "Yes, Mrs. Dayman, Kazzim, he will be in school, tomorrow. Thank you. Thank you, Jake."

Jake's Mom smiled at him and gave him a giant hug as they walked to their car. Jake knew that at ten he couldn't change the events of the world, he couldn't change what had been forever changed, but he could help to change Mr. Habib's feelings, even if for just a sort while, and he felt as if he had really accomplished a lot for one day.! And by the look on his Mom's face, he had!

They said their goodbyes to Mr. Habib and Kazzim, and got back into the car to go home again. As Mrs. Dayman pulled away from the curb, with her flag flying from the window of her car, she smiled and looked over at Jake. "Jakie, you really are an awesome kid, you know. You did a wonderful good deed, today. You did exactly what we all have to do to get through this tragedy. You, Jakie, you did just what being American means. I'm so proud of you, sweetie."

"Thanks, Mom. It made me feel good, too. Mom, do you think things will ever get back to normal? Back to the way they were?"

Jake watched his Mom as she struggled to answer him. "No, sweetie, I'm sorry to say no. I don't think things will ever be quite the same. Too much has changed. But we will have to come to terms with it, come to accept it and do the best we can with what we have. That's what you did, today." Sherry Dayman paused, and then smiled, "Let's go home and put your special flag up at our front door."

"Good idea, Mom, good idea." Jake actually felt himself smile a real full smile for the first time in two days.

Afterward

You may wonder why I chose to write a book about a Fifth-Grade boy and his two days during the Attack on the World Trade Center. I wrote about Jake for several reasons. I was a Fifth-Grade teacher, and I was in my classroom with my students on Tuesday, September 11, 2001. The twenty-six students and I lived through the tragedy together, and we will never forget where we were or what happened on that day. I will never forget the looks on their faces and the many feelings that I felt toward them. I will never forget the way that my attitudes about teaching and the children changed and grew dearer to me on that day. I began to look at my Fifth Grade Class of 2001-2002 as very special children who had lived through the biggest and perhaps the most important change in their lives, although they weren't really mature enough or old enough to understand the repercussions to come. We all felt a certain bond to each other that was hard to explain and which we didn't really express in words. I began to place much importance on what I was teaching them and started to place more importance of morality issues and feelings for those around them.

The Fifth Grade "privileges" that Jake looked so forward to were factual. However, because of the 9/11 events, the school district that I taught in cancelled all of the planned trips into and around New York City, as a safety precaution. How sad it was for the children who I taught, who had so looked forward to seeing "The Lion King" on Broadway, to face the canceling of their long-awaited trip. This was probably the first and most tangible effect that they felt on themselves. Fortunately, we had no casualties in my class, although others did suffer.

My class did make one large flag for the hallway as a combined project with another class, and we talked endlessly about our feelings. They also wrote a wonderful book, which they titled, The Day You'll Never Forget, 9/11/2001. It is a collection of historical facts, essays, letters and poems written from their dear hearts. Each child received a copy to be brought home, and it was good therapy.

Jake was a combination of many of the children in my class that year, my own children when they were that age and students I had worked with in other years. Most of the events were what had actually happened in my classroom that day and the next. The phone calls, the fear of the future phone calls, the lockdown, were all real. My two sons and my daughter-in-law did work in Manhattan and our cousin did work at Windows on the World and she was actually late for a meeting that day! Of course, the events about the actual attack were all real and presented in the book as they actually took place.

Mr. Habib was a fictional character; however, my morning ritual was to stop for a giant coffee every morning on my way to school at a local chain convenience store. It was there that I saw the look on the faces of the employees whom I had seen each and every morning for years, many of whom were Middle Eastern, and so I decided to incorporate them into one character, Mr. Habib.

What happened in the days, weeks, months and years to follow the attack on the World Trade Center and America was at the least very difficult to comprehend and to live through. Its saddened inhabitants had come to grips with the aftershocks of the tragedy that had befallen them. The world mourned the loss, and New Yorkers lived it daily.

Ground Zero loomed and would loom larger than life forever, as hallowed ground, as hearts were heavy and forever changed for all of the families and friends and coworkers of the NY Policemen and women and New York's Firefighters who lost their lives. We mourned the thousand of those who worked in the Twin Towers and still remember them formally each year, although they are forever lost by their families and friends.

Once it was crystal clear that there would be no miracle in finding survivors, Ground Zero became a shrine and a monument to the tragedy of lives that were lost there. Innocent citizens, firefighters and Policemen were all hailed as heroes forever. New York City's bravest became the bravest in the world. People found solace and comfort in visiting and placing flowers, notes, letters and pictures there to those who lost their lives, which was very much similar to the way the children in my class felt about writing their book. Patriotism, as Jake saw, was heralded and a newfound sense of it became vogue. Flags and pins and the wearing of the red, white and blue were everyday occurrences. People were kind and polite to each other and mindful of things like opening doors and saying thank you.

Soon after 9/11 came the Anthrax scare as another form of terror threatened us when anthrax-laced letters were sent to members of the United States Congress and people in the media. A new form of fear spread once again. People were afraid to open their own mail, trips for vacations and family occasions were cancelled, as Jake's Grandparent's trip was. And even that didn't seem to be much of a sacrifice.

When I first completed this book in 2003, we were still at "war." Life and hope did continue, however, for most of us. My class finished their book and felt a great sense of accomplishment. Although they didn't get to take their trip to Broadway to see "The Lion King," they enjoyed other local trips and laughed and carried on as Fifth Graders do. They had their Fifth Grade Dance and picnic and "Moved Up" from Fifth Grade to a new school. And they learned everything they were supposed to in their required curriculum and a larger-than-life lesson about humanity and love for each other and love of their country. We would never forget where we were that day, Tuesday, September 11, 2001.

As I write this it is September 2014, eleven years after September 11, 2001. I chose to work on my story once again because time has passed, and the new Freedom Towers loom larger and taller than the Twin Towers have been built at the site of the World Trade Center, ready to open and house thousands of New Yorkers at their workplaces. I felt this an appropriate time to pay tribute to them and to allow young readers to read, feel, learn from and understand what happened on that ground eleven years ago and to pray to keep our new occupants safe and sound.

*One World Trade Center is the name of two buildings. It most commonly refers to the primary building of the new World Trade Center complex in Lower Manhattan, New York City, and the tallest skyscraper in the Western Hemisphere.

Nina Mittman- 9/2014

It is now September 2025 and I just reread my book, which has never been published. I think it may be the right time now!

www.ingramcontent.com/pod-product-compliance
Lightning Source LLC
Chambersburg PA
CBHW062024040426
42447CB00010B/2118